Things n' Stuff I know About Massage:

Blurbs, Rants, Raves, and

Riveting Tales from the Bodywork Industry

By Raf King

AKA The Five Crying Tigers

Dedicated to

My beautiful wife, Linda Marlana King.

Thank you for blessing my life with your existence.

A big thank you to

Raul Garcia, Bryce "TC" Richards-Garcia, Wendy King, Katherine Williams, Michel Williams, Frankie Almonte, Summer Shipley, Visnja Robovic, Leroy Youvella, Jennifer Craig, Chelsea Miller, Kristen Willingham, Sheri Hines, John Hines, Jolene Christal, Mark Yochum, Justin "Apache" Cue, Paul Ledoux, Jim Dunaway, Alysha Gurule-Willey, Maria McKraken, Chris McIlquham, Christy Martin-Kuratko, Keith Kuratko, TJ Fritz, Mike "Get your house keys" Gasiorowski, Jeremy Raetz, Katie Reed, Kris Marler, Darci Nakagawa, Denise Patch, Jennifer Roseman, Matt Faulkner, Shadrach Miller, Dr. Danielle Miller, Dr. Justin Gehling, Dr. Oryan Salberg, and Dr.'s Tiffany and Jerome Longoria…much love to you all. Thank you for your guidance and inspiration.

Specials thanks to

Jacob Holly for the cover art.

Denise T. Pinto for contributing her art – 'All of a Sudden'.

Declan Cooney for his musical contribution.

Linda King for her contribution to the art in this book.

Raul Garcia, Bryce "TC" Richards-Garcia, Wendy King, Katherine Williams, Michel Williams, Jennifer Roseman, and Matt Faulkner for their edits.

You are all truly amazing at your craft.

To my reader:

I rant a lot in this book, but I do not speak poorly of the client. I love all my clients and your privacy will be respected. In fact, I've left a plethora of stories out simply because a client was involved and didn't want anyone to feel weird. If you're a massage client picking up this book, you don't have anything to worry about. This is meant as a tool for you—whether you're an aspiring massage therapist or a client this is meant to educate you on massage therapy and give you insight into my career and experience.

Now, if you're a corrupt employer I worked for, a shady colleague I once worked with, or a student (both awesome and less awesome, I love all my students regardless) then there's a good chance I mention interactions we've had in these pages. But even then, I limit the number of names mentioned—of people and of businesses both. It's not my intention to hurt anyone's reputation or damage their income, most of the people from these stories are plenty good at doing that themselves. But again, this book is a tool meant to educate the reader on massage therapy and give insight into my personal experience.

Also, of course you have the table of contents, but here's a short guide for you, as well. Part I is about how I came to find this path and some educational material on massage therapy. Part II is about my experience with massage education and is continued in part IV. Part III involves more of the strongly positive and wildly negative sides of my career; this is where the book really starts to get juicy. Part IV revolves around frequently asked questions and short stories. Part V is a secret—only for those who brave the first four parts! Mwauhahaha! Enjoy!

Also…there's some foul language in here. '*Sentence enhancers*', if you will. Sooo… viewer discretion is advised.

Table of Contents

PART IV – Ouroboros and the Titan's Hunger

PART V – █████████

Now, let our journey begin for the five crying tigers.

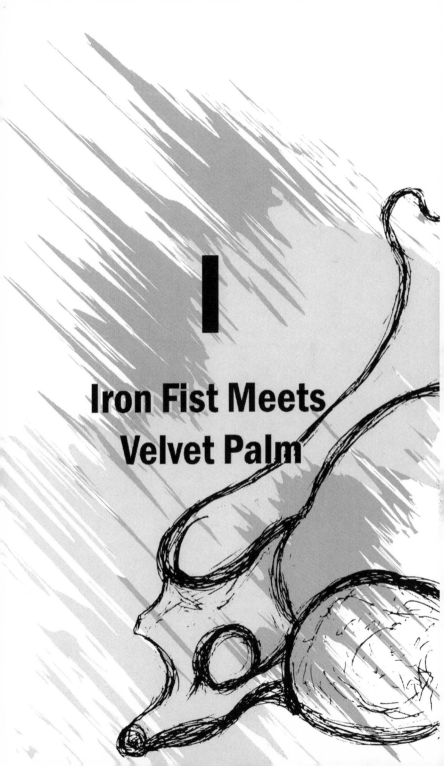

I

Iron Fist Meets Velvet Palm

Who is Raf King and Why Did He Become a Massage Therapist?

A head-on collision with a drunk driver didn't break my father, but it came damn near close. The impact created enough force to flatten the front of both trucks. It happened in my early teens and I stopped seeing my old man smile. He was left with multiple herniated disks in his low back and arthritis began to ravage his entire spine shortly thereafter. The doctors gave him pain medication to manage his pain, only to result in more frequent and heavier doses. Eventually, he was taking 260mg of morphine every night just to make it through work. Then, it got worse.

He started to have an adverse reaction to the morphine; a terrible rash would break out over his entire body. So, every night he would have to choose between paralyzing pain or wanting to tear his skin off. The doctors couldn't offer surgery due to the condition of his spine and didn't see any other options for him. He lived like this for years.

Then one night, I fell asleep on the couch watching tv and had a fever dream. It was so vivid—I can still feel how real it was. It was raining and all the buildings around me looked like a Tim Burton movie set. Flat, jagged, and black. I was on my knees in the middle of the street holding my father as he slowly melted away in my arms. He didn't say anything, but he had this look in his eyes, "*Why couldn't you save me? Why didn't you do more?*" I saw regret and helplessness in his eyes. And just as his body completely liquefied, I awoke to one of those old, cheesy commercials for the massage school. They mentioned something about being able to manage pain in clients and I was sold. I didn't need to hear anymore; I knew I needed to act. No one else was going to do anything, it came down to me. So, the next day I went down to the school and signed up for a year-long program. That was back in 2008.

It was a hell of a rough start. The people in my life were actually fairly confused and disappointed in my decision, at first. My father, a special forces marine, didn't understand. He hadn't heard of massage as a viable therapy and didn't get why I was choosing this path. My stepmother said I would never touch her. My siblings made fun of me, my girlfriend dumped me, and my friends quit hanging out with me. Also, and this was the kicker, the average working years of a massage therapist before their hands gave into arthritis is three years. Three years of using my hands before I couldn't anymore. *What the hell am I getting myself into?* But I pushed forward, I had to do something for papa. I took it day by day, sometimes hour by hour. Weekdays consisted of 4am – 12pm work, 1pm – 4pm study and practice, leave for school around 6pm, get home around midnight, sleep for a few hours and start the process all over again. On the weekends I did my clinical internship and eventually started working another part time job too (all while somehow trying to balance and fit working for a band in there as well). There were times I called this journey my "Battle of Thermopylae" (the battle from the movie 300) as I knew there would be no retreat. I accepted this might swallow me whole, but I'd give all I had before it did. "To the cliffs!"

Another big influence for me were the words of Alexander the Great as he pulled up to shores of those to be conquered, setting his own ships ablaze, "We go home in the enemies' ships, or we don't go home at all." As in, there is no safety line here, there is no point in retreat because it will only lead to certain death. The only way out is through, into the belly of the beast.

Over the course of that year, I practiced on my father every day, and eventually he even came around to the idea. And by the time I had graduated, he was able to take his pain medication from 260mg of morphine to nothing. He still needs maintenance every now and then, even till this day. But now he smiles. Now, he's got a chance. And now, he doesn't rely on pain medication that makes him want to rip his skin off.

After completing that program, I signed up for an advanced program to further my skill set. I figured at this point, with the results we had gotten from my father, I ought to try and be the best and make a living out of it. As I finished the second set of courses, I started working in spas and clinics around the Phoenix area and eventually landed a job at the school I graduated from as a teacher's assistant. It wouldn't be long before I would climb the ranks to an instructor's position. I spent years there. I loved that job and it was heart breaking to leave the education environment, but I now run my own mobile massage therapy company with my wife—Living Kinetics Mobile Bodywork. We travel to peoples' homes, to care facilities, to sporting events, offices; wherever we're needed to perform our craft. I'm happy to tell you that I'm living my best life. It was no easy ride, but it was well worth it.

I feel like every moment of my career has been preparing me to be a business owner. Sometimes I kick myself and whine about not having started my own practice earlier in life, but the truth is I had to experience poor working environments and greedy owners so I could do the exact opposite of them. I know exactly what not to do while running my business, which has given me a lot of clues on what I should be doing.

So, who is Raf King and why did he become a massage therapist? He's just a guy who didn't want to see his dad in pain, and now doesn't want to see you in pain either.

Massage Techniques and the Bipolar, Schizophrenic Field

Massage therapy is a culmination of many origins and different styles of bodywork. There really isn't one right way to do it, but there are plenty of wrong. It's because of these many origins and the creation of new styles that we see different languages and attitudes spark into modalities. Not only is this chapter set up to talk about the different nomenclature and philosophy in massage and how unaligned it is with itself, but it's also meant to prepare you for the rest of the book. I may use some of these terms later and don't want you to be lost. And, I mean… "*it's pretty cool…pretty, pretty cool*" (name that reference and receive your very own, FREE pat on the back!).

There are five classic strokes of Swedish Massage, and one of those is broken down into two distinct parts, so basically six. Of these six strokes, there are multiple hand positions and alterations you can make for each to truly create an arsenal of techniques that are unique to you. Swedish massage and its associated strokes are normally what the media attempts to portray to you. This style usually utilizes fluid motions with long, connecting strokes and focuses on a slower tempo. So, without further ado, please allow me to introduce to the classic strokes of Swedish Massage:

1) Effleurage

>Translates from French, "to skim", is probably one of the strokes you think of when you think of massage therapy. These are the long gliding movements that you see in all the movies and ads. This technique ranges from light to deep pressure (then called deep effleurage for the technically savvy) and is often used to relax the nervous system and increase circulation in a local area. This is also a fantastic 'connecting' technique, meaning

it integrates segments of the body to help make one feel whole and one.

2) Petrissage

Translates from French, "to knead" (which is quite common word play in the massage field. Interchanging 'need' for 'knead'). This is a technique that pulls the muscle away from the body to work it—imagine a farmer and a cow utter. That same sort of pulling and milking motion can be used on certain muscles, like the biceps, and can help increase blood flow and with the elasticity of the tissue.

3) Friction (gliding)

Put your hands together and rub them back and forth. You've just successfully completed your first attempt at gliding friction. This quick gliding motion across the skin is gliding friction. Fantastic for bringing blood flow to an area and increasing fluid exchange in joints.

4) Friction (non-gliding)

Still friction, but on a deeper level. Let's refer back to our hands rubbing back and forth to produce heat, now imagine deep muscle layers performing something similar (but not as exaggerated). Basically, by not sliding on the surface of the skin but still generating a small movement, you encourage the act of friction into deeper muscle layers. In some cases, there is no movement, we call this a 'compression' and sometimes it's exactly what the body needs. Non-gliding friction techniques are great for reducing knots and scar tissue.

5) Vibration

Much as it sounds, its vibration. Quick, short movements with the hands while maintaining contact with the body. Vertically or horizontally on a specific spot or shaking

6

an entire limb. Great for interrupting pain cycles, relaxing a segment, and increasing blood flow. This technique has also been shown to help with bone fractures, hormone production, and increasing muscle mass, but we'll talk more about that in the 'Benefits of Massage' chapter.

6) Tapotement

Translates to "tapping" from French. This is a percussive stroke that utilizes different hand shapes to produce different impacts along the surface of the body. From using the fingertips, to cupping the hand and using the palm, to using the sides of the hand (like a relaxed karate chop).

Now that we've got those Swedish names down, let's follow the theme of the chapter title and explore Russian massage techniques. Some names are reused while their application changes, and other names stay the same. Russian massage prides itself on being a rhyme and reason type of modality, thus has more of a 'recipe' type of approach during a session. Also, with a segmented flow and more moderate tempo, a shorter stance and shorter strokes are normally used. Allow me to introduce the strokes of Russian massage:

1) Effleurage

Just like the effleurage from Swedish massage, but only refers to a light application. For example, when you're applying lotion.

2) Wringing

Just like effleurage from Swedish massage, but only refers to a deeper application and is normally a shorter stroke that doesn't act to connect segments of the body. For example, applying a deep gliding stroke from the wrist to the elbow, instead of wrist to shoulder as a Swedish practitioner might do. (Please note, that the Swedish modality also utilizes a technique called 'wringing' that actually resembles the motion of wringing out a towel and isn't just a deeper, shorter effleurage. Bonkers right?)

3) Petrissage (pulling)

Just like the petrissage from Swedish massage.

4) Petrissage (pressing)

Non-gliding friction from Swedish massage.

5) Friction

Gliding friction from Swedish.

6) Vibration

Still vibration.

7) Percussion

Swedish tapotement with a name change.

Now, let's just talk a little neuromuscular therapy, or what a lot of injury rehabilitation clinics will incorporate into their work. All the same nomenclature as its Swedish counterpart, with the exception of:

1) Friction (gliding)

I've heard a lot of neuromuscular massage therapists use the term 'gliding friction' to describe their deep gliding techniques (deep effleurage and wringing). I think this is a play on Swedish's gliding friction but done at a much slower pace with greater depth. The term 'stripping' has can also be interchanged with this movement as well.

So, as you can see, there are a lot of different names all trying to describe the same thing OR names that describe a variety of things. I mean, there're four different names for a 'deep gliding' technique. The Swedish terminology is used most in the field, but in the process a very useful Russian application can be overlooked or even lost. Many haven't heard of Russian massage or Russian Sports Massage, but even in that regard, many massage therapists that do sports massage still use the Swedish nomenclature. So, it is and isn't what people refer to when talking about sports massage. Are we seeing the problem here yet? Let's pile some more on top while we're at it.

Neuromuscular vs. Myofascial vs. Structural Integration vs. Rolfing vs. Other cool names for modalities

I've heard these terms a lot in the massage world. Neuromuscular literally means muscles and nerves, myofascial translates to muscle and fascia (connective tissue), structural integration IS Rolfing but changed its name and guess what: works with fascia—these are all just fancy terms that describe specific parts of the massage world. Sure, some of these modalities require differences in pressure, speed, draping, technique, and body mechanics, but all in all they're still just describing bodywork. Good ol' fashioned bodywork (the exceptions being more medically based massage, especially those that deal with cancer). But, what's with all the names?

There're a couple reasons for that: 1) Practitioners genuinely want to focus on one aspect of the field and want to ignore the rest. I personally think this is a limiting mindset, but many prosper because of it. "Absorb what is useful. Reject what is useless. Add what is essentially your own." –Bruce Lee. Notice the quote doesn't say "absorb what is useful, from one source", just absorb what is useful. If you have found a single source of infinite knowledge and wisdom that works for you, kudos to you. But keep in mind, this quote comes from a man that mastered dancing to become a better fighter. Learn what you can use, even if it looks different. Moreover, this is the same guy that believed systems of martial arts SHOULD change and look different from person to person. "We are always in a process of becoming and nothing is fixed. Have no rigid system in you, and you'll be flexible to change with the ever changing. Open yourself and flow, my friend. Flow in the total openness of the living moment. If nothing within you stays rigid, outward things will disclose themselves. Moving, be like water. Still, be like a mirror. Respond like an echo." –Bruce Lee. 2) Because it costs less. Getting certified in Rolfing or Active Release Therapy (ART) costs thousands of dollars, and that's just for one half of the body. It's way cheaper to turn in the paperwork to the board (or not) claiming a new modality and practicing that instead (almost like putting goofy glasses and a mustache on it and passing it off as something new). Even big companies do it. When I was in massage school, 'Rolfing' was called 'Structural Integration', 'Active Release Techniques' were called 'Call for Movements', and 'Hot Stone' was called 'Hydro Stone'. And I know there's at least one massage therapist reading this and just squirming over the small details between this and that, but let's get real for a second—those details probably aren't great enough to justify an entirely different name.

But here's inherently the problem with lots of names: lots of confusion. More names describing similar techniques means less communication from therapist to therapist and even less from the client. Moreover, it negates variants of technique by creating a vagueness on how to name or expand a technique. Also, it's harder to know what the client is supposed to ask for— are we in the personal service field focused on the spa life or are we to be integrated into the pain management field to focus on movement? This is a common back and forth in our industry and many encourage the divide. I personally feel this falls into the 'two sides of the same coin' category and you should be able to deliver both but nonetheless, it still creates confusion. So, because of all these names, massage therapists must learn multiple languages to communicate experiences from the client, and even then, they might be learning dead languages.

It's kind of like when students would get to the 'injury massage' class in school and people thought we were going to redefine everything they learned up to that point—nope. It's just basic massage with the acquired knowledge of injuries and pathologies to go with it. It uses all the same tools, just with the slight twist of knowing what can further harm or help the client. The true magic lies more in the critical thinking of your practitioner, not some five-finger-floating-lotus-healing-palm technique that you learn after so many classes that cures tendonitis specifically.

For this field to not only thrive, but just even survive, we need to at least try and get on the same page with each other.

History – Let's Clear Something Up!

Per Henrik Ling isn't the "fAtHeR oF sWeDiSh MaSsAgE". He opened a gymnastics school and taught some of his closest students some massage techniques. They even made up their own names; that of which we didn't even talk about in the last chapter—that's how much impact he DIDN'T have on massage and its nomenclature.

I'd be more inclined to referencing Johann Mezger as the father of Swedish (or rather modern day) Massage. He rooted massage therapy in science and even coined the most common terms, still widely used today. He named them and proved they do something medically sound; he gets to be the father.

I taught at a school where they VEHEMENTLY believed Ling to be the greatest thing since sliced bread. (Like no joke, I debated three other instructors on this subject and all they could say in the end was they hadn't actually read the course material and didn't know what they were talking about. Yeah, stay tuned for some fun/depressing stories with them.) NOW, I don't mean to insult Ling, look, I even capitalized his name, but teaching wrong history has always been one of those things that's kind of irked me. Yes, he does have a cool story and you should check it out (he was sick and traveled to find a cure), but he's not what's taught in most massage schools. He did use massage to manage severe ailments. He did teach other people about massage. He even helped bring it to the States. Totally was Swedish too. But Johann Mezger had named, proved, and popularized Swedish massage in a way that Ling didn't. Moreover, Mezger didn't just popularize massage, he reinforced that it was a modality to help the sick and injured—through science! (I hope you read that last line with your best 'Dexter's Lab' voice) Massage wasn't just massage anymore; it was massage **therapy**. ALSO!! Mezger named these classic strokes in French to further emphasis their nobility, which we still use today. I can almost guarantee you, you haven't heard the nomenclature from the Ling system.

I almost like to think of this scenario like Thomas Edison and anyone who produced a light bulb before him. He wasn't the first (seriously, by like 77 years!), but the light bulb he produced was cost worthy and efficient, thus it was able to be mass produced and ushered in a new era. Although people had tinkered with the idea of the light bulb before him (in fact, before he was even born), he was the start of commercial manufacturing for this product and would have a far greater impact on society because of it.

Yes, clearly at this point, one could lecture me on the meaning of "father" and could also probably debate my statements, but what's really the point? —of titles I mean. Sure, it probably feels nice to be called as such, but it just leads to cult followings and a lack of reasoning in the long run. It's in these types of mindsets that we end up not being able to question the teachings, skill, or character of a prominent figure. I see it a lot with Bruce Lee. You can be a big fan of his and love his influence on cinema and martial arts while still questioning him. In fact, if you've read his philosophies, he wants you to question him and everything else you see. But over and over I hear someone ask if Bruce Lee really was a good fighter or just a convincing movie maker, and 'real' fans lose their minds over it. *"How dare you question the late and great Bruce Lee!"* Don't get caught up in the worship of an individual, it suppresses your reasoning and therefore your skill. Because worse yet, this idea expands into something even more sinister: once you believe someone to be infallible, then you believe everyone else by comparison to be wrong—always. It happened at the school from time to time, entire cohorts would fall for one instructor and ignore the words of the rest of the staff. All you achieve with this is cutting knowledge off from other avenues. (By the way, fun fact about me, I'm also not really into the title 'master' either. It's normally used in a way to imply you have nothing left to learn. While to the contrary, you can now simply learn with a whole and new perception. We could get into a full discussion here about limiting yourself and the Dunning-Kroger effect, but I think we'll save for that another time.)

But while on the subject, I find it even stranger that John Harvey Kellogg is rarely talked about in the discussion of modern massage, he's often just mentioned as side note. He was kind of like an American Mezger, in a way. He organized a system to "eliminate the unnecessary and inefficient, and to develop and perfect those methods capable of securing most definite and prompt results." (Art of Massage, 1895) And yes, it's totally the same guy you're thinking of—the inventor of corn flakes! (Which BTW! Fun Fact! Mr. Kellogg was very religious and apparently condemned sexual activity of any kind, even with his own wife. He originally invented corn flakes as a suppression for sexual desires, particularly masturbation. So yeah, enjoy breakfast with that in mind.)

But way before these three dudes were the fathers of massage and way before light bulbs were ever even thought of (like seriously, like thousands of years), China and India had already explored massage and other modalities. These forms of bodywork would evolve and influence the entire region. (BTW, totally had a student once call me a racist because I mentioned the system of acupuncture had moved from China to Japan influencing the practice of Shiatsu. She was a weird gal. Like I said, stay tuned; we'll talk more about my interactions with students and other folks here in a bit.) My point being, although these three men are important, there's so much more history to massage and bodywork than Mezger, Ling, and Kellogg—don't get caught up in celebrity worship.

The Benefits of Massage

This book has a lot of whining and negativity in it—let's talk about some cool, upbeat stuff; the benefits of massage. There are so many wonderful ways that bodywork can affect you. In this chapter we'll go system by system through the body and briefly discuss how massage can benefit it. Let's get started ☺

Integumentary System

The skin can definitely be impacted by massage therapy. Any stroke that glides over the skin is going to create an exfoliation effect, which is awesome! The removal of dead skin cells isn't something we normally think about when improving our health, but the act of removing that dead layer of skin can lead to more efficient sweating and waste excretion. More sweating will lead to keeping a more consistent body temperature during movement. Also, I've noticed a change in attitude after someone exfoliates. It's kind of like a mini purge for the body.

But what about non-gliding strokes? Even still we see a benefit! Strokes that don't glide along the skin will improve elasticity of and circulation (all massage increases localized circulation, btw) to the skin. This has been shown to increase oxygen absorption. Crazy how our skin can absorb O2, huh? Well, it's not very much, like 1 – 2% of what you need, but during athletically charged events, you need all the oxygen you can get. Let's draw our attention back to that word "elasticity"— do you mean like having stretchy skin? Well, yes and no. Your skin should have a healthy turgor to it. Meaning, it should stretch and then go back to its original form after stretching. Without the ability to stretch, skin rips. Without the ability to reform, skin sags. We know that massage can help with the stretch, now let's talk about the sag.

Percussive strokes are great for reinvigorating tissue, especially the skin. Early in my massage days, I had an instructor that would religiously tap all around his face for five minutes every morning. After a while it became a game to try and guess how young he was because he kept such youth over the years. You could look at a series of photos of him over a decade and he barely changed in appearance. You know, kind of like…a vampire. *Come to think of it, he really only taught night classes.* You should try it though, the percussion not vampirism, it's an active way of fighting wrinkles and loving yourself. Besides, what's the worst that can happen? You look a little silly in your restroom, alone, each morning? Not so bad, some of us look silly no matter what we do.

Musculoskeletal system

Let's move onto the meat and potatoes of massage: the musculoskeletal system. Now, really, this is like three systems: muscles, bones, and joints (and one might even argue connective tissue, but we're going to talk about that separately).

Muscle pain is probably one of the biggest motivators for receiving massage therapy. Tight muscles can lead to nerve impingement which can lead to more pain. Moreover, tight muscles can also hinder other systems as well. For example, hypertonic muscles can restrict blood flow causing an area to become ischemic. In other words, this system is very important to take care of and massage is a perfect fit. Let's talk about some of the other ways bodywork can benefit your muscles.

Gliding type techniques will encourage blood flow to muscles and the pressure will also induce a lengthening effect in the tissue as well. This combined with non-gliding and percussive type of strokes can improve muscle tone, contractility, stamina, flexibility and even reduce spasms and cramps. In fact, petrissage, percussion and vibration have all been shown to encourage muscle growth and recovery from an injury. As in, if a muscle becomes atrophied (shrunken in size) due to lack of use, these strokes can help with the hypertrophy (mass building) process and cut down on healing time. During the 1980's, Russian scientists found that their cosmonauts could spend more time in space when a whole-body vibration device was used (modern versions are available for purchase). The lack of gravity lead to atrophied muscular tissue and a vibration machine would combat that and a list of other side effects as well.

Massage can even help with bone health. It's more specific to the use of vibration and percussive strokes, though. You see, the vibration and percussive effects on the body encourage the stimulation of osteoblastic activity which will work to rebuild bone. So, if you are recovering from a fracture, old Russian massage manuals recommend performing five to ten minutes of vibration per day. Most massage therapists use their hands to perform this technique, but if you were expecting a duration of five to ten minutes, then I would recommend using a mechanical vibration device instead.

But what about the joints? Again, absolutely. This has a lot to do with fluid exchange and providing ample nutrients for the joints. Gliding friction and percussive strokes are great for joint health. Both do a radical job at increasing localized metabolism. You can try it yourself right now, put the book down and rub your palms back in forth over one of your knees really fast for like three seconds. Then make flat hands, move the tip of your thumbs to match the tips of your fingers, and pat around the same knee for three more seconds. How does one feel v. the other? I'm sure you can feel a difference, and that was just six seconds. Imagine how'd you feel after an hour session.

Fascial System

The connective tissue (fascia) of the body seems to be overlooked in a lot of conversations, but it should be talked about as a system unto itself. It really is 'majestical' (I'll give you a high five if you can name that movie)—in fact, if I could only study one system of the body, it would be this one. Yes, all your systems are important and are all beautiful in their own way, but if you could only study one system, then this would be the one that could give you insight into all others and help you understand the body in a whole new way, as well. Connective tissue wraps around every muscle cell and blends those cells to bone, it encases all your organs and anchors them, it can reshape itself due to daily habits, it even ensures you don't explode during movement (okay, so that's a bit of an exaggeration on my part, BUT you should really check out some sweet articles that talk about how much pressure you generate internally during a lift and what kind of stress that puts on the horizontal bands of the body. Ever wonder why the beer gut looks the way it does? You have a band of connective tissue that wraps around and reinforces you, much like a weightlifter's belt. Obviously, without this support, you can run into some big problems. This is really just a side thought for anyone interested) and here's the coolest part to me: it's all interconnected. It's all one piece. It's easy to consider how the circulatory or nervous systems travel throughout the body, but here's the big difference: The shape and continuity of the fascial system defines how we move, and this shape can be changed and repatterned. That's amazing to me! This interconnected system defines our kinetics and our movement through this life, but we can decide how this tissue is shaped and what it defines for us. Think about this: did your mother ever tell you to stand up straight? Of course, she did. But why? Because practice makes perfect. They more you put yourself in a static position or perform a repetitive motion, the more the body adapts to it. Ever see someone who sits a lot throughout their day try to walk or stand? It's not usually fully erect standing and you'll notice they kick their legs forward to walk. These are both compensations for a body that's repatterned itself to a seated position.

Often when we think of movement, we think of muscles. And when we think of muscles, we think of individual compartments. Your bicep is not your hamstring. They're all individual mechanics working together, but that's just it, connective tissue is that thing that helps all this work together (and yes, a properly working nervous system helps out too). So,

18

when you genuinely start to think about how the bottom of your foot is connected to the top of your head, it can be kind of mind blowing.

But how can massage help this system? Massage can be a wonderful tool for encouraging the elasticity of this tissue. Remember that whole repatterning conversation we just had (being in a seated position for a long time and adopting the posture)? Well massage can help break that holding pattern. We mentioned that connective tissue has some contractility to it, which means we can help it relax—we can help it lengthen. Holding a segment in a twisted/stretched static position, deep gliding strokes, and deep non-gliding strokes can have a wonderful impact on short connective tissue. I'd even ask your massage therapist about Gua Sha therapy—it's like a scraping technique, SO GOOD! (side note – I remember when I was going through school learning about rolfing/structural integration and we were working on the calcaneal/achilles tendon. The person I was working with had a C shaped tendon due to poor posture and letting the foot collapse while standing—after just two strokes we already saw a drastic change in alignment.)

But let me be very clear here, massage therapy should not replace movement when trying to realign and lengthen the connective tissue of the body. MOVEMENT IS KEY! Getting a massage once a week and then changing none of your daily habits will result in minimal progress and resentment towards your massage therapist. Learning body mechanics and how to move can most definitely have a positive impact on your day. I'm talking like, making huge leaps of progress in minutes. No one teaches you how to move, you just copy the people you're closest to. You copy your mother and father's holding patterns. No joke, look at pictures from when you were a toddler and compare them to pictures of your parents. You probably both put all your weight on one leg, and both have the same hip hike. It's kind of like finances, it can have a drastic impact on your life and overall health, but it's rarely taught to any of us or if it is, it's like way late and you've already formed some weird habits.

19

Did anyone else have to change their amazon prime password so their spouse would quit ordering stuff?

But let's talk about one more *really* awesome way that massage can help out with connective tissue: scars. Scar tissue forms when damage has been done to the body. Kind of like a patch. Now again, to be clear, mindful movements from right after an injury occurs to after the scar tissue has set is key. Proper movement will influence scar tissue fibers to align with muscle fibers, versus looking like a spider web. Spider web like fibers aren't good for movement, but they are for stability. The body is just trying to protect us, but keep in mind, it only thinks in the short term. It doesn't care if you'll have joint problems when you 80, but you should.

So, we've established once again that movement is key. But what if you have trouble moving? Or what if it's a scar that may not impact movement, thus won't be reduced by movement? Two kind of extreme sides of the coin but this is when massage can help most. So, if you can't produce movement, then massage may be a wonderful additive to your treatment plan. It can help reduce scar tissue via deep non-gliding strokes (think like scratching a really deep itch). Even simple range of motion techniques can give you a head start in the right direction. And as for superficial scars on the skin, I probably should've covered this more back in the integument section, but yes, regardless of the age of a scar massage can help reduce it in size and appearance. You could even do this alone at home. Without lotion, repetitively glide over a scar of your choice (think gliding friction). If its new, glide with the fibers, if its old, glide against them. Be sure to take pictures to document your progress!

But is there ever a time when scar tissue shouldn't be broken up? Yeah, sure. This might be one of the hardest lessons for new massage therapists to learn. We're led to believe in our schooling that we have to eradicate any and all knots and adhered tissue, to relax all muscles make and create length, and

MASSAGE IS THE GREATEST THING EVER!! GAAH!
YEAH, YEAH, YEAH! PILLS BAD, MASSAGE GOOD.
ROO, ROO, ROO! Which is kind of the point of school, it gives
you a chance to fully immerse yourself in a topic and put it on a
pedestal. But here's the thing, massage has its limits just like
anything else and you have to remove the ego and respect that
before truly treating someone. I remember when I first graduated
from school, I thought massage was the answer for everything.
Wanna lose weight? Massage. Wanna run faster? Massage.
Wanna blah blah blah? MaSsAgE. And massage can assist with
all these topics, yes, but there are way more effective methods
out there that will get you there faster. Massage, as amazing as it
is, has its limits.

So, when don't we break up scar tissue? If a muscle has
fully detached itself from the bone, then later reattached itself via
scar tissue, you shouldn't break up that scar tissue. You can still
massage the area, but our focus isn't on disrupting the body's
solution for reattaching a muscle. In fact, this may not even be
the time for you to play your role. If that person did want that
changed, they would need surgery. Massage could drastically
help with the recovery process post-surgery (same day, even!)
but it wasn't necessarily the initial answer to the problem. This
part of the book isn't meant to put massage down, but rather just
a reminder to all massage therapists out there to play towards
your strengths and work towards what's best for the client.

For more info on how amazing your connective tissue is,
I recommend you check out a book called "Anatomy Trains" by
Thomas Myers—it's truly fascinating stuff.

Side note – My thoughts on cranial sacral and other light touch
modalities.

Referred to as "the lazy man's massage", Cranial Sacral
(also craniosacral) Therapy is often portrayed as a light touch
modality that can cause radical changes in the organization of

connective tissue, move bone, and can affect mental and behavioral health disorders (you should also do some reading on the 'cranial sacral rhythm' which refers to the very, VERY small expansion and contraction of all mammalian skulls). It primarily focuses around the head but is used throughout the body. Think like the weight of a nickel, that's how much pressure is being used to alter connective tissue length and mental behaviors. Very subtle and non-invasive.

Often, when we think of pressure, we also combine the concept of depth as well. "Light, medium, and deep" are normally the choices you get when selecting what kind of pressure you'd like in a massage, but "deep" doesn't have to necessarily mean "heavy" or "a lot" of pressure. It can just mean "deep". To clarify, it makes sense to put the two concepts together, almost like harder and faster—they naturally go hand in hand. But for a moment here, imagine depth without pressure. Here's an example to help: a pendulum. Think about how you would begin to generate a swing. After the first few, smaller initial movements, you gain momentum and eventually space out longer movements. And even though the end of the pendulum may be moving far more than it was before, you aren't necessarily generating tons more force. In fact, the portion of the pendulum moving the most, is furthest away from where you are holding. It's within this mindset that much of cranial sacral therapy comes from.

BUT! How does Raf feel about it? Cranial sacral therapy and other light touch modalities have their place, and that should be respected. No modality is a one size fits all when it comes to results. BUT! I have used this style before and seen its benefits. Although I'm writing about this in the connective tissue section, it could also have been brought up in the nervous system section, as well. For you see, this modality can change how a person acts and thinks. All from depression to schizophrenia. My brother growing up had to deal with ADHD issues, but any time I used cranial sacral on him, we noticed a difference. I still remember the time he said in a super chill voice, "my head doesn't feel like a part of my head."

Double side rant – Unwinding

Unwinding is a technique that was taught to me during my advanced cranial sacral training. As you begin to undo holding patterns and lengthen bounded connective tissue, you can encourage the body into an auto pilot mode and have it perform a continuation of the technique. This normally involves unconscious movements and even emotional responses (somato-emotional responses can be common in bodywork, but especially with this modality. They normally come in the form of laughing or crying). Kind of like learning how to ride a bike, you might have someone there to support you at first, but after some time you understand peddling and take off by yourself. But then there's the next problem: how to stop.

So, imagine this, we're all in classroom practicing this new technique, the air is still and some light music plays in the background. After a few serene moments, it happens. People on the tables start moving unconsciously—these are movements the body needs to 'unwind' or unbound tight areas, but it doesn't look natural. At first the movement is subtle, a slight jerk or spasm, then that evolves into contorting and moving in ways you didn't know a body could.

Then the laughing and crying started. That untamed laughter. Those echoing cries.

I wasn't prepared for this at the time, seeing people pretzel up all the while switching from tears to laughter. It lasted like this for three days, for some.

I know I'm painting a dark picture here of the event and that's really just my attempt at comedic relief, but please, I do encourage you to check out your local cranial sacral therapist and see if an unwinding session is right for you. Everyone in my class that did unwind that day all ended up feeling much better afterwards. So, don't let me deter you. Okay! Next section!

Nervous System

Massage and the nervous system dance beautifully together. Some might even say the two main drivers of massage therapy stem from effects in the nervous and cardiovascular systems (coming up next). Changes in this system can create a butterfly effect throughout the body. The nervous system is your communications relay, you might think of it as your electrical wiring. Massage has the ability to stimulate or sedate the nervous system, depending on technique and desired outcome. But why would you want either of these?

Let's start off with sedating the nervous system. So, there are times when the mechanisms of the body can work against itself and create a feedback loop—a chronic pain cycle. Let's consider this for example: you're stressed at work and because even though our brains are evolved, they still can't tell the difference between work stress and being hunted by a lion stress, it manifests the same. One common side effect of stress can lead to your shoulders rising, much in the sense of an angry animal raising its shoulders and lowering its head. It seems as though this is part of the response: protect the neck and all its vital parts because something 'bout to go down. So, you're stressed, your shoulders raise, this goes on continually because we've somehow tricked ourselves into living modern life like this, knots begin to form in the shoulder muscles creating headaches and sending pain down your arms, this in turn leads to more stress which that continues the cycle. "*Oooh...he's sensitive.*" Oh no, let's go with this one, "*Back in my day we were lucky if we got knots and we were grateful when we did!*"

When this happens one the best things to do is encourage the body to go through a bit of a reset (almost like your modem at home). By doing a lot of slow, rhythmic, predictable techniques we can help the nervous system relax. Of course, working out knots and treating the short tissue will also aid in breaking the chronic pain cycle.

side rant –

Often when massage therapy is discussed, its broken down into two categories: relaxing and therapeutic. This is for amateurs. There are so many massage therapists that think "specializing" in a modality means making it hurt—that it can't feel good or relaxing anymore because it's for pain management. And yeah, there are definitely times when a treatment becomes intense, particularly when an injury has just occurred. But to make it your focus seems like you're cutting yourself short. I've definitely had people fall asleep on me while working the psoas (deep abdomen), subscapularis (in between scapula and ribs), and sternocleidomastoid (the front of the neck) muscles. And if I can achieve that, I know any other massage therapist can too—really, I'm all thumbs. I Don't know how I made it this far. So, quit thinking of yourself as one or the other and understand the tenants of both, only then will our clients really receive the full benefit of our work.

But now back to our anatomy meets massage discussion, why would you ever want to stimulate the nervous system? Well this can come in two different forms: stimulating the central nervous system (CNS) and stimulating the peripheral nervous system (PNS). Let me start with the CNS, your brain, like waking someone up. We don't often think of massage to stimulate someone, but take for example, I used to try and massage my dad before he left for work (night shift) and this was to ready his body for movement. Yes, you should warm up before lots of movement. No, massage doesn't normally replace that, but we had to work with what we had. And for out intents and purposes (*intensive purposes! Haha!*), that nightly massage was supposed to act as a warmup. Naturally, the outcome could not result in a relaxed client, but a stimulated one. This means the massage therapist should be using a faster pace, having a less than predictable flow to the strokes, and should normally rely on more pulling, pressing and percussive techniques—not many gliding strokes, particularly because you don't want to use lotion or gel for the treatment. If they're getting ready for a physical event, they probably won't have time to shower and why risk altering how they sweat with lotion/gel/oils on the skin?

The coolest part of massage and the nervous system comes in the way of neurotrophins. These are the specialized proteins specific to nervous tissue that induce function and growth. For many years, it was widely believed that nervous tissue did not regenerate after being damaged, but recently that thought has changed. There's been evidence of 2 – 5mm per day of nervous tissue regeneration. Massage can give the body the chance to double those numbers. Massage can strengthen a weak nerve single by stimulating the release of neurotrophins. Feel free to check out The National Center for Biotechnology Information's website as it has some fantastic studies that show how vibration in particular can influence this process. Touch alone can help stimulate nerve function and growth, but it seems as though vibration really takes the gold when it comes to stimulating the regeneration process of nerves.

And as for developing nervous tissue, yes, infants can benefit from massage, as well. Touch is crucial to the survival and development of a child. Without nurturing touch, some children won't just lack in development but can even pass away. I remember reading this horrifying article while going through massage school about a severely understaffed orphanage. Only some of the children were held –all were fed though. Every child that wasn't held regularly passed away.

On a less dark note though, infant massage and nurturing touch can almost super charge your baby. *superhero music plays in the background* As your child grows and adapts to their surroundings, a lot of changes are happening. One of those changes is the myelination of the nerves—think insulation of wiring for your communications system, much like your wiring in your home and appliances. This insulation causes nervous signals to work fast and more effectively. How this wrapping is set up causes 'saltatory conduction' to occur. *Sauter* in French means to jump and that's very much what's happening along your nerves. The insulation leaves gaps of non-insulated area, this forces chemical reactions to occur and in turn help push the nervous signal. Think like a bucket brigade. The buckets of water move much faster when being passed from person to person in a line rather than one person walking from the source to the fire. Why is this important? Ever heard of multiple sclerosis (MS, remember Montel Williams?)? This is the unwrapping of your nerves which can lead to a lack of an ability to speak, move, feel, or anything else your nervous system is in charge of. Getting massage early on and frequently won't save you from MS but it will deter its effects. Even if this unwrapping occurs, if you develop more myelination as a child you won't feel the effects, as quickly, as an adult.

Cardiovascular System

Really, any massage stroke is going to increase localized blood flow—massage is all about circulation. Whether its effleurage encouraging blood back from the extremities, or its vibration conditioning the circulatory vessels with its quick compression movement, or its tapotement's rapid percussive invitation of nutrients—massage is all about circulation. Some might even say health is proportional to blood flow. The more blood flow you get to an area, the greater chance for oxygen, fluid, and nutrient exchange to occur, and the more those exchanges that occur, the better chance you have of healing or maintaining health. The body is fantastic at maintaining circulation, but that doesn't mean it can't use some help at times. Especially when an injury is present. Much like the nervous system, when we affect blow flow, we create a ripple effect of healing throughout the body.

Digestive System

The digestive system isn't something we normally think about when the benefits of massage come up, but boy oh boy, let me tell you, there are some wonderful benefits to be had here. Overall better blood flow to the area will of course help with nutrient absorption, but massage can also help condition and strengthen the smooth muscle used by the organs. 'Peristalsis' is the movement utilized to move matter through—think like squeezing toothpaste out of a tube. Vibration is an excellent technique to help with this and can definitely aid in our next topic as well.

Let's not forget about constipation! I'm sure we've all experienced it at some point. My brother had many digestive issues growing up and constipation was just a normal part of life. Getting some non-gliding friction/pressing petrissage along the large intestine can work miracles. As weird as it sounds, with this technique you're breaking up the matter in the colon and allowing for a smoother transition process. Hey, c'mon now, everybody poops—or at least everybody deserves too.

Now, you may have noticed that the abdominal area normally isn't included in a full body massage. This is mostly due to time restraint. Most clients would rather spend time working on other parts of the body. Other setbacks might include draping (moving the sheet to uncover a part of the body) and overall comfortability for client and practitioner.

Naturally, we always protect our clients' modesty in a massage, so extra draping is required for women. I try to treat everyone the same, but it's much easier for men to refuse, or even laugh off, a towel across the chest. Some massage therapists may have not learned this type of draping (or even forgot it over time), so they may avoid the area altogether due to lack of trust in their skillset. But this also plays into out next topic: comfortability for client and practitioner.

For the client, having the abdomen exposed can add a degree of vulnerability to the session, which is already present to begin with. We would have to have a special talk the day before abdominal massage class to avoid sharp declines in attendance. The belly is naturally an emotional place (some even say this is where your second brain is!) and society has led us to judge our value against how this area looks. There's a lot going on here for the client already, and it's easy to skip the area because of it.

For the massage therapist, it's easy to skip areas that they aren't confident with or areas that aren't asked about. Although working in this segment can have wonderful benefits for the rest of the body, your massage therapist may be waiting for you to inquire about it. It's easy to get into a routine that works and then not modify it (I know I've had my days). Communicate with your practitioner and ask if abdominal massage is right for you.

Respiratory System

Another system we don't often think of when the benefits of massage come into conversation (which I know naturally happens all the time for everyone) is the respiratory system—breathing. The benefit of this system more so falls under other categories, such as muscular and nervous. If you sedate the nervous system and relax the intercostal (rib) muscles you can allow for much bigger, more fulling breaths. This will in turn increase oxygen uptake which is needed particularly if you live an active life.

But it doesn't just stop there—in this book I've also mentioned how massage can affect your bodily awareness. Posture plays into this. If I present with rounded shoulders and a large arch in my upper back, then there's a good chance my diaphragm doesn't have its full range to expand and contract, meaning more shallow breathing from the chest instead. Overtime, bodywork can help with this.

And let's also consider short tissue and knots can reduce range of motion and enable poor posture. Let's take our abdominal muscles for example, by lengthening the abdominals you'll encourage the rib cage to sit at a more level state. In other words, bodywork won't just help with bodily awareness, it will also help break the bad habits and speed up the good.

Lymphatic System

There's an entire modality of massage dedicated to this system. Suffice to say, the lymphatic system can be heavily aided by massage therapy. But what is it? In short, it's part of your immune system and is a series of vessels surrounding your blood vessels that fights infection and removes foreign bodies. This is normally when swelling can occur. Unlike the other series of vessels in our body, the cardiovascular system, the lymph system doesn't have a pump (the heart), it does have some smooth muscle to help with fluid movement, but naturally, lymph fluid drains with movement and exercise. You are designed to move and heal, as backwards as that might sound. But what if it's too painful to move? What if you just don't have the energy? Massage can be a wonderful assister at this point to help manually move the lymphatic fluid, this is called lymphatic massage.

Normally this type of massage is light with short, repetitive strokes and at first glance might not appear to be doing much at all, but it can have quite the impact and can be exactly what the body needs. In fact, heavy pressure may actually 'close off' the point of fluid movement and exchange in lymphatic vessels. (This is yet another reason why I don't box myself into just one part of the field. Some massage therapists only train to give deep pressure and it shows. Your technique should be just as consistent from light to firm, from fingertips to elbow, from your first session to your last.) Be sure to ask your massage therapist about lymphatic massage and see what it can do for you.

But please, I do invite you to try a beginner's treatment for yourself at home. Next time you're in the shower, try washing in segments with lymphatic flow—basically brush towards the heart, segment by segment. For example, try washing from elbow to shoulder, then wrist to elbow. Knee to hip, then ankle to knee. You get the picture. Always brushing towards the heart. This light movement along the skin is roughly the amount of pressure a lymphatic massage uses and roughly the same pattern as well. Even if you're not suffering from excessive swelling, good lymph flow can keep you from getting sick and also increase your daily energy.

Endocrine System

Rarely (like never) does anyone come to me asking for work on their glands. No one is ever like, "Hey, can you work on my thyroid for me? Then work on my digestive glands afterwards?" That just doesn't happen. When there are issues with hormones and glands, I normally turn the client's attention to an acupuncturist or western doctor, not massage. BUT, that doesn't mean massage techniques haven't been shown to affect the endocrine system and the expressing of glands. In the early 80's there was a team of Russian scientists that were experimenting with the effects of vibration and found that when performed on the site of a gland for at least five minutes (no longer than 10), you could stimulate activity and secretion. More so in the glands of the gut, but nonetheless this means you can trick this system into working harder with this technique.

Reproductive System

Much like in the previous category, no one's coming to me asking to help with their reproductive system—and if they do, they might be asking for something not so therapeutic. *Ha! Gross!* But I do have a story that fits the bill: I had an instructor during my massage training that told us he got a client pregnant. Of course, he purposefully used that wording to grab our attention. What he meant was he was working with a woman that had some serious hip issues and they were doing a lot of anterior hip work (psoas and iliacus muscles) to help correct the problem. She was also actively working with her husband, not the massage therapist, to get pregnant, but with no luck. After the hip issues were addressed and no longer bothering her, the happy couple conceived. Naturally, the theory became that because the connective and muscle tissue were so tight, it was disrupting how the fallopian tubes functioned. So, by lengthening the tissue in the abdominal area and front of the hip, the tubes were able to work more efficiently, and the rest of the process could occur.

Now, I don't know the legitimacy of this story and I personally question the credibility of the instructor (he was fired from multiple campuses), but it doesn't sound completely irrational to think that creating life requires certain conditions and massage helped with those conditions. As with all things in life though, reason with it and you be the judge.

Success Stories and What I've Seen

Although I've mentioned stories with my father and brother in this book, I have to be very careful when it comes to clients' personal information and accounts. HIPAA (Health Insurance Portability and Accountability Act of 1996) ensures a degree of privacy for our clients and patients. Naturally, we'll always take our clients and their information seriously, but HIPAA is an ironclad assurance that the common person will be protected when seeking help. With this in mind, we'll be keeping this brief: I've been practicing massage therapy and bodywork since 2008, and since then I've seen countless cases do complete turn arounds because of these treatments. I've seen people move without pain after living with it for decades. I've seen athletes put 50lbs onto their lifts just after weeks of working together. I've seen mean men smile and I've seen hopelessness fade.

And the personal success stories go both ways. I've grown so much as a human being during my time as a massage therapist. I CRINGE when I think about how I used to treat people, how I used to view them (which isn't bad, it just means you've grown and will never go back). When I first got into the massage field, I took everything personally and judged people by how they looked—I didn't bother to detach myself from a situation and look deeper. Kind of like looking at a leaf and missing the forest.

I remember the first real growing experience I had at a clinic. I met a man; he was a rude man. There's a brief interview you do before a massage therapy treatment, and he gave me attitude the whole time. We had only gotten part of the way through the questions before he said, "C'mon guy. What? You never been on this side of it before?" Implying that I didn't know what massage was like or what I was doing. So, I cut the interview short, left the room to let him get on the table, washed up, composed myself (I took the interaction personally, I do believe the appropriate term for how I was acting was like that of a 'snowflake'), and started the treatment. I folded the sheet over to expose his back and noticed these cute, little tattoos on each of his shoulders. Normally I don't ask about clients' tattoos, but I just had to this time. And he explained in the nicest voice that each tattoo was picked by a grandchild and they got to pick where it would go too. I felt terrible. In an instant, I realized that this wasn't a brute—this was a caring, loving grandfather that was in pain and needed help. He wasn't trying to be rude, that's just how his communication works when he's in pain.

I met another man with a giant symbol of hate tattooed on his back. He was a nice man and took zero objection to my brown skin. I suspect it was a mistake of his former self; people change, sometimes even for the better. It seems like there are ebbs and flows to loving and accepting humanity, but all in all because of my time as a massage therapist, I am more caring, more receptive, and overall more patient with those around me.

"All you need is love, love is all you need." –The Beatles

What Should You Ask Your Massage Therapist About?

Here's a brief chapter on some topics that I feel are heavily overlooked in the bodywork world. Some topics that you may want to ask your massage therapist about next time you see them.

Desk worker/driver with headaches - SCM

Do you have headaches and work at a desk/drive for your job (or really any occupation that sets you in one position with your head forward)? Ask your massage therapist about working your Sternocleidomastoid (SCM) muscle. This muscle sits in the front of your neck and not only helps rotate but also pulls the head forward, like when you're looking at a monitor (or driving or doing basically anything in front of you). It's the ropey muscle that connects from your clavicle and sternum (Sternocleido = sternum-clavicle) to the just behind your ears (that pointy part of your skull is call your mastoid process). The name just describes its attachments. Now, most times when headaches are brought up to massage therapists, they automatically work the back of the neck and the shoulders, which isn't wrong, I just don't find it to be a complete treatment. The SCM muscle can contribute to poor posture of the neck by pulling the head forward, this will in turn make all the other neck muscles tight. Think about this, your head plays a balancing act on your atlas, or 1st vertebra. This can be likened to balancing a bowling ball on two fingers. It takes all sides and muscles firing to keep something like that balanced. Too much this way and you're forced to compensate. Overcompensate and you have more problems. This is why the massage therapist must be complete and thorough with their work around the neck. Without *completeness* you may just be alleviating problems to create more.

Also, keep in mind, the knots, or trigger points (TrP), that can form in this muscle will DEFINITELY give you headaches. The headaches can present behind the eyes, and on the top, sides and back of your head. These areas can overlap with pain referred from the trapezius muscles, or shoulders. In some cases, even jaw pain. The worst thing about knots are, the pain it sends to remote areas of the body can in turn create more knots, that also send pain. So again, if you're not complete with your work, you may be perpetuating a problem.

Many massage therapists will shy away from this area (the front of the neck) because of the delicate structures present (nerves, blood vessels, trachea), so you may have to ask about it. I do encourage you to find someone that is comfortable in their anatomy and has experience with this area.

Some of the best results I've gotten with this muscle stem from Proprioceptive Neuromuscular Facilitation (PNF), a form of stretching, so please do ask your massage therapist about that as well. It's a basic technique that most practitioners should know, if not, here's a brief explanation for you: 1) Stretch an area as far as you can. 2) At end range of motion, resist. Gently press against the stretch for five to ten seconds. (e.g. Bending over to touch toes and stretch the hamstrings, step two would involve doing the opposite of touching your toes and trying to stand up as someone presses down of your back to resist.) 3) Relax. Some feel at this point like they need to go return the limb to its normal position, this is fine. Or you can simply move onto to step four. 4) Take stretch further, WITHIN YOUR COMFORT ZONE. And it's that that simple, just rinse and repeat from there. The contraction in the middle of your stretch can do wonders for convincing the body to lengthen.

It's because PNF plays off the safety system of the body. You have little sensors throughout your joints and muscles that detect when you're going to fail. They help detect when too much stress has been put on a tendon or muscle and can help prevent joints from being hyperextended. When these sensors start firing, you may automatically or instinctually perform an action. Ever been handed something waaay too heavy? I'm sure your first reaction was to drop it. Anyone ever push you into a stretch too fast? I'm sure your first reaction was to resist it. Muscle and connective tissue become wary when tissue has a drastic amount of stress put on it quickly, and it will do its best to protect it. But it's within that protective mechanism that we can also help the body let go.

This technique can be used just about anywhere on the body. Do your homework, do your research, and ask your massage therapist about PNF stretching. It could be a game changer for you.

Desk worker/driver with upper back pain – pecs, major and minor, and serratus anterior

If you have upper back pain and work at a desk/drive for work, then you should ask your massage therapist about working your chest, anterior (front) shoulder, and rib muscles. The pectoralis major and minor and serratus anterior muscles. Obviously, there are so many more muscles that contribute to this, but here's a starting place for us. These muscles mostly sit in the front of the body and pull the scapula forward, rounding the shoulders, like when you're developing a dowager's hump (or in layperson's terms: a hunch back). It's very common for this posture to occur, due to our daily activities. All these muscles help perform actions in front of you, which most of our day calls for, thus through repetitive use and poor habits they can become short.

Pectoralis major, is the big obvious musculature of your chest. The term "pecs" normally refers to this muscle. It connects your arm and rib cage and allows you to create a hugging type of motion. Pectoralis minor (the little brother), is the ropey muscle that connects from your shoulder (acromion of scapula) to ribs three through five. If you feel around through your pec major muscle and press deep into it, just inferior (lower) to your clavicle, you'll be able to feel it. You may have a hard time

37

finding your serratus anterior muscle, but if you press and slide your hand high along the ribs, you may feel some tender tissue. This is more than likely it, or at least part of it. Only a portion of serratus anterior is superficial on the ribs because it travels up between the ribs and scapula and attaches to inner (medial) edge of the scapula. This is important because not only does this muscle contribute to poor posture and upper back pain, but, through poor diet and lack of movement, this muscle can glue itself to the scapula and ribs. You know how you feel first thing in the morning, and you have to do a big stretch? Imagine parts of the body that never get that stretch or any movement at all, eventually they stop trying. 'Adhesive capsulitis' is a term that encompasses that very set of symptoms.

All these muscles either pull the scapula forward or round the shoulders in. So, when these tissues become short, it puts the back into an overstretched position. Meaning this, an overstretched area can also feel painful and be full of knots and SHOULD be massaged, however, you always want to address the cause as well. The knots forming in your back are attempting to stop you from continually rounding the shoulders leading to a more compromised spine. Knots in muscles get a bad rep, but in some cases, they are trying to ensure the integrity of the body. When a joint dislocates, knots start forming to help hold onto whatever possible and deter further loss. Moreover, plenty of knots will form after the joint is set as well. The body wants to ensure stability.

Now, most times when upper back pain is brought up to the attention of the massage therapist, they automatically work the back, which isn't wrong, I just don't find it complete, yet again. Just like with the SCM muscles, the pec muscles and serratus anterior muscle can contribute to poor posture, which of course affects other structures creating a cycle if left unaddressed.

Let's talk knots and these muscles. So, in a general sense, the knots from pectoralis major and minor and serratus anterior can send pain: down your arms, to your upper back, and across your chest. Your upper back may hurt, and you massage it, only to get minor, temporary relief because without being complete with the work, you're bound to perpetuate the problem.

Many massage therapists will avoid this area (the chest and ribs) because it can require additional draping for female clients and often this area can be very tender and sensitive. But as always, I do encourage you to find someone that is comfortable with their anatomy skills, draping skills and can work in this area.

BONUS TIP! One of my favorite exercises is the 'rhomboid activation'. I'm sure there's a number of ways to do this, but here are my instructions:

1) Lay on your back with your knees bent. Bring your arms out to your sides, in the 'T' type of pose, with your palms facing towards the ceiling.

2) Pull you scapula (shoulder blades) together and keep them pulled together.

3) With your shoulder blades still actively being pulled together, bring your palms together. Do this 3 times.

4) After those 3, turn the hand so the thumbs are facing up towards the ceiling. With your shoulder blades still actively being pulled together, bring your thumbs together. Do this 3 times.

5) After those 3, turn the hand so the palms are facing down towards the floor. With your shoulder blade still actively being pulled together, bring the backs of your hands together. Do this 3 times.

6) Stand up and enjoy how you feel.

Desk worker/driver with lower back pain – psoas, QL's, and glutes

Do you have lower back pain and work at a desk/drive for work? Ask your massage therapist about addressing your Quadratus Lumborum (QL's), glutes, and psoas muscles. Basically, your lower back, hips, and abdominal area. Obviously, there are so many more muscles that contribute to this, but here's a starting place for us. These muscles either attach directly to, or in some way influence the position of the lumbar spine.

The QL's are small square muscles that attach to your 12th rib, pelvis, and lumbar spine. Feel that small space in between your rib cage and pelvis? That's where these little guys (or gals?) are at. Because of its fiber orientation, it can definitely affect the spine.

Self-care side note – I'm not a big fan of the foam roller, but I do see its effectiveness on the legs and upper back, but I would recommend alternating the foam roller for a lacrosse ball in the low back instead. Back to more anatomy and massage!

The psoas muscles sit deep in your abdomen, in front of your spine and connect from the spine to the inside of your thigh. This muscle is a deep, core muscle responsible for bringing your knee to your chest and turning the leg out. It also influences the curvature of the low back. If you are in a seated position often, this muscle can become short and when you go to stand, it will draw the lower spine too far forward creating discomfort. You may not even stand fully erect because of it, but rather slouched, with a forward head position and rounded shoulders to compensate. It's very common for this posture to occur, due to plenty of work revolving around the seated position. I'm even writing this book while sitting. Tsk, tsk. Kudos to you if you alternate between sitting and standing!

Something else to note about the psoas, however, is it may not be a problem with how tight this muscle is, but rather how weak it is. A weak psoas will give you just as much trouble as a tight one. Here are a couple of tests for you to tell the difference:

1) Lay on the edge of your bed and with one knee pulled to your chest and the other hanging off. If the leg hanging off the edge floats in the air as you lay back, then you probably have a tight psoas.
2) Stand up and again, bring one of your knees to your chest and balance on the other foot. Actively keep your knee at your chest and let go of it. If it drops then you probably have a weak psoas.

The awesome news is, both of these tests act as exercises too. You can repeat them to gain length or strength in the psoas muscle. I also recommend you check out a talented personal trainer if you are experiencing a weak psoas muscle.

The glute muscles don't directly attach to the spine, but they will affect the position of the pelvis and therefore, have a tremendous effect on the low back. You have three sets of glute muscles: maximus, medius and minimus. Maximus makes up the large, obvious portion of your rear (in the same sense the pectoralis major makes up a large portion and shape of the chest). Medius and minimus sit more laterally (to the sides of) then maximus does. Think about the parts of your hips that really make up the bottom half of the 'hourglass' shape. It's these muscles here that will unconsciously fire in a way to level the pelvis. So, if you sit for long periods and with a wallet in your back pocket, you are purposefully off setting your pelvis, and just like we learned with the upper back, knots will form to save you from yourself. If you offset the pelvis, the muscles around it will tighten up, creating a vicious cycle. Tightness trying to correct tightness. If you are suffering from sciatic pain, then definitely work these muscles. Your sciatic nerve roots from the lumber spine and sacrum and these muscles can severely impact the health of that nerve.

Let's talk knots and these muscles. So, in a general sense, the knots from QL's, psoas, and glutes can send pain: down your legs and to your low back. Meaning this, you sit too much and knots form in your psoas, low back, and hips. Knots in your low back and hips create more low back pain and eventually tighten your legs up, tight legs lead to lack of support and your low back is affected again. It becomes a vicious cycle fast.

Many massage therapists will work the QL's and glutes no problem, but many will avoid the abdominal area because it can require additional draping for female clients, has delicate structures and often is tender and sensitive. I've even met some experienced massage therapists who say it's too dangerous to work. I don't agree and am confident in my technique. But it can be rather cumbersome to work for both client and therapist. But there is a happy medium! There's a way to work the psoas without directly working on it. Remember reading about PNF stretching with the SCM muscle? Its absolutely perfect for this muscle and highly recommended. Be sure to ask your massage therapist about it. And if you've picked up anything from reading this chapter, I'd hope it be that you should find someone that is comfortable with their anatomy skills, draping skills and can work in this area.

BONUS TIP! If you've worked through a lot of what I've mentioned already, ask your massage therapist to check your calves. There's a mean knot that can occur in the soleus muscle that, unlike other knots, doesn't send pain further down the extremity but rather up it. This knot in your calf may be transmitting pain to your lower back. Check it out.

When Not to Get Massage

GASP! You mean there's times when you shouldn't get massage? Well, kind of but not really. There are times when you should completely avoid massage treatments, times when you should just avoid an area, and times when you just need to change the approach. These are called full and partial body contraindications (contra = not indicated) and don't always mean 'stop' but rather 'caution', and even if you can't get massage now it probably won't be forever. Talk to your massage therapist before the treatment and be sure to communicate. In many cases, if you manage your condition it won't have any effect on the massage. Common examples include but are not limited to:

Times to avoid completely (full body contraindications)

Fever

> This one is debated in the field. My personal feelings are *"yeah, that's gonna be a 'no' from me dawg."* I've heard the argument of 'flushing out' the infection but I just feel the body is already taxed by doing its job of containing the virus—the bodies temperature is already elevated, and massage can risk increasing it more. No 'sage.

Contagious conditions

> Although steps are taken to sanitize after each and every session, if there's a chance that a serious disease can be transmitted because of the treatment, then we have to avoid it.

The spread of an infection

> Not from a contagious standpoint, but rather within the client's body, if there's a chance to further spread or mobilize a disease by working on any part of the body then massage should be completely avoided (such as a

43

blood clot or cancer. Now, cancer is what I call a 'general contraindication', meaning, the general practitioner will probably not possess the knowledge or skill to properly help, but one with specialized training will. This is one of those cases where you need to find someone who specializes in 'oncology massage'.).

Under the influence of drugs and/or alcohol

There are three reasons to avoid or alter treatments when dealing with drugs and alcohol:

1) Massage therapy has a fantastic effect on blood flow. With this in mind, if you have a substance in your system, whether it's prescribed or recreational, will reflexively filter through your liver at a faster rate during a massage. Not only can this be taxing on the liver, it also can affect time released medication or the duration/impact of its effect. Talk with your massage therapist, it normally comes down to scheduling your appointment at the right time of day (e.g. before your take your meds or after so many hours). Really, it's no biggie.

Now if its alcohol, just don't mix alcohol and massage, period. I know how nice it sounds to get drunk and get a massage, but its normally a recipe for disaster. Clients that do drink and get bodywork normally report feeling nauseous during the session and sore the next day. Even some reports of projectile vomiting mid-session (I've never experienced this, but oh god, the stories, oh god). This is probably due to increased blood flow and filtration leading to a faster, and more intense 'peak' (hello spinnies, here we come!) which also leaves you dehydrated too. I've had clients in the past have a drink before a session and nothing bad happened. But it can be a fine line and I don't recommend you flirt with it. Don't mix alcohol and massage.

2) The effects of a medication needed to be accounted for. You may have to adjust a treatment because of what that particular medication is doing for the body. For example, if you're prescribed blood thinners for your heart, then you'll probably be more prone to bruising. Getting a deep tissue massage while on blood thinners is not recommended, but you can still do lighter, more gentle types of bodywork. I'd suggest asking your massage therapist to add more range of motion techniques and probably stick to shorter, lighter sessions. Medications have all types of effects on the body and understanding those effects will better aid the massage therapist in tailoring the session to each individual client. Which leads me to our third and final reason to avoid or alter treatments when dealing with drugs and alcohol.

3) If sensation is altered, and proper feedback can't be given. I had an instructor that told me a story of when he worked on a lady who had just taken some Vicodin (a pain killer) and kept asking for more pressure—he ended up snapping one of her ribs. The crazy part is the medication was working so well, she didn't even notice. Your massage therapist doesn't want to hurt you, but without proper communication and feedback from the client, your risk for injury increases. Now, I think this conversation slightly changes when we're talking about someone with nerve damage and we're using touch to stimulate a response and growth. But even then, it's not deep and vigorous massage. Its gentle and short in duration.

Compromised Immune System

I read this a lot in massage literature. But I feel this is a category that should be altered, not avoided. The approach should be changed. Maybe shorter, lighter sessions and always making sure sanitization protocols are being followed. HIV/AIDS falls under this category and the infectious disease category—is it double trouble? For the client, yes, for practitioner, no. The client is far more at risk for injury in this situation. Much like before, the massage therapist needs to take a gentle approach and make sure sanitation protocols are being followed. By the way, this does not necessarily mean the use of latex gloves. At times, gloves may be used during treatments, but this doesn't have to be one of them. In fact, if you feel you do need gloves because of an open wound present on the client (blood to blood contact is how this diseases transfers) then you should avoid the area or massage completely.

Loss of integrity and sensation

As our bodies age, they break down. It's a natural part of life and a part we should all try our best to delay. But just because you're aging doesn't mean you have to skip out on your massage. Much like all the other advice I've given in this chapter; shorter, lighter treatments and always be aware of what risks there may be. Several examples include:

> Thinning skin – leave out quick strokes like gliding friction and do less twisting/rotating types of techniques.

> Osteoporosis (thinning bone) – requires lighter pressure.

> Arthritic joints – may require assistance when moving and extra bolstering.

> Loss of nervous sensation – requires more feedback and a gentle touch.

I had an amazing instructor when I was in massage school who gave me some great advice, "No matter how great a technique is, you have to ask yourself if the person receiving it can handle it.

If they can't handle it, then it's not a good technique. Always be aware of the integrity of one's body." (Thanks TJ!)

Times to avoid an area (partial body contraindications)

Open wounds

> I'd hope this one is pretty self-explanatory. Please don't rub other people's open wounds. In fact, just don't rub any open wounds, not even yours.

Brand new tattoo

> C'mon, it's basically an open wound.

Rashes

> If it is exclusive to a local area, then just avoid that area in most cases.

Surgery

> Another debated topic in the world of massage therapy: surgeries and when is it okay to start massage treatments. Of course, surgeries come in all sorts of shapes and sizes, and each one person reacts uniquely to the process—but I feel massage can be a strong support in the recovery process from a surgery and should be involved. Obviously, the massage therapist should not be using deep or vigorous techniques at this point, but I feel you can start massage therapy treatments directly after surgery, same day even for some. Now again, shapes and sizes, some patients require rest after a surgery but my point being, some massage literature says to wait up to six weeks minimum before starting treatments.

> Naturally, this debate comes down to the patient talking with their doctor and figuring out with them what the best course of action is.

As always, talk to your massage therapist before the treatment and make sure you're both on the same page. And if you'd like more info on contraindications and massage therapy, I'd recommend books like "A Massage Therapist's Guide to Pathology" by Ruth Werner, "Pathology A to Z: A Handbook for Massage Therapists" by Kalyani Premkumar, and "Step-by-Step Massage Protocols for Common Conditions" by Charlotte Michael Versagi.

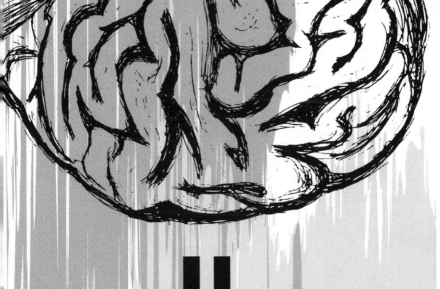

II

From Student to Sensei

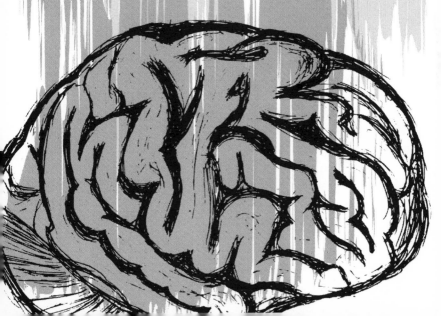

Who Becomes A Massage Therapist?

The coolest. Or laziest. I actually don't know. I see many paths lead to this industry, but it's really the people with unconditional love in their hearts that *continue* to be massage therapists. There are a lot of "average career span" studies I've heard of for practitioners in this field, and they normally don't expect people to make it past five years before arthritis makes it impossible for them to work. I know people that have been doing this for 30+ years and are still going strong. The universe is a strange place, but one thing that seems to be near constant: you get out what you put in. Express love and receive love.

Students of the Massage School

There are many types of people that would come through the massage program, so it's really not fair to put all students into categories because there were just so many individuals that were there. True individuals. And it was an honor to be a part of their education process. However, there were some notable groups that we can talk about: the "lotion pushers", the "career hoppers", the "hobbyists", and the "hardcore healers".

The Lotion Pusher

Much as the name sounds, this is a person who signed up for massage looking for an easy career. Who could blame 'em? A big part of massage school marketing revolves around the idea of working less and making more money. So, it's natural that people looking for an easy paycheck would show up. Normally after they find out they have to learn about anatomy and injuries, even on a basic level, they start dropping like flies.

There's even a smaller group within this group: the lotion pusher with rich parents. At the end of the massage program, it was asked that all the students do a presentation over their experience and where they see themselves in so many years. And without fail, every class had at least one kid that would say, "I'm only here because my parents said they would stop paying for [X] if I didn't get into a school…so, I don't really plan on doing this…?" Which should really show you, massage school wasn't that hard unless life was throwing some real curve balls your way. I know some students that went through absolute hell to finish the program.

The Career Hopper

I have a lot of admiration for the people in this group and much as the name sounds, this is a group of individuals going through career changes. Often, this category of student is made up of older folks who have spent many years working a job because they had to and are now finally able to pursue something because they want to. This can look different for many—for some it's because they've saved enough and are retiring but for most it's because they reached an end point at their last career. A burn out point. Regardless, it's not easy going back to school after so many years of doing something you know. It's not easy being in the education environment, period. There's a lot expected of you and it's on your dollar. It's inspiring to be around someone who will brave the unknown and place themselves in such a vulnerable position. I think a more appropriate name for this group would be the "reinventors".

The Hobbyist

This is the type of person who joins massage school because they already have a fantastic career but are looking to bring some tried and true technique to some of the massages they do for their spouse or friends. They normally have a knack for hands on work and are looking forward to a professional educational experience. (fun fact: I went to school with man that joined so he could give his wife good massages. Owned his own business and was living a good life. Halfway through the program she cheated on him and they got a divorce. At this point, he was already too far into the program to avoid the big bill and she destroyed his business. It broke my heart hearing about such a noble action being spat on. Okay, so maybe not such a 'fun' fact.)

Now, you would naturally think that the hobbyist would be easy to get along with. Massage isn't all that hard and they normally aren't worried about grades or minor point value differences. And for the most part, sure, they didn't give me much trouble, but there was always one that would occasionally pop up and thought because this was a hobby for them, that they didn't have to participate or follow any rules at all. Instant. Headache.

The Hardcore Healer

Of course, massage therapy doesn't heal the body, it merely encourages the body's natural healing process. But you know that type of person who just screams "shaman healer"? Like, they have a different presence about them—it's almost intimidating at first. The kind of person so present in a conversation that you feel listened to for the first time in your life. These are the kinds of people that have been giving their parents massages since they were young and just get it. It was always so humbling to have this type of person in class. Not only did I get the satisfaction of helping a person reach their goal but being around them made me realize how much better I could do. I'm not the kind of guy that massage came naturally to, it took a lot of hard work and dedication, but seeing gifted folks reminds me to not try but do.

What I Wish They Would've Taught Me in Massage School

Hospice Care

No one ever mentioned that massage therapy goes great with hospice care. So, of course, they never mentioned how to cope with it either. That's easily the hardest part of the job for me, being there at the end of someone's life. My hat goes off to anyone that has to see life passing on a daily basis—this world doesn't deserve you. But although the work can be taxing on the soul, luckily, it's also incredibly rewarding as well. I've met people that never had a massage before they were put on hospice care and seeing their face after they made such a discovery is moving. Regardless of how late they discovered it.

For me, I barely experience what many others do. But something that makes the job harder is not being notified when someone passes (I contract with a hospice company and I'm low on the chain of command and sometimes am overlooked in operations). I show up for their scheduled appointment, and a loved one has to mention it. It's hard to come up with the words for what it's like being there in a moment that raw.

What gets me the most though is when they apologize—either the client or their loved ones. God that fucking kills me. When they say sorry because they're getting on the table late or because we had to cut the session short or because there was a mix up in scheduling; it just rips my heart out. I don't ever want to hear a person in their last days or their loved ones apologize for what they think is inconveniencing me.

It hits hard when they're young too. My age or maybe 10 years older at times—it scares the crud out of me. Seeing an older folk pass that lived a long successful life and built a legacy, although sad, still has a certain natural sense around it. But seeing a young person dying boggles the mind. Death comes for us all, we know this, but must it come when there's still so much to see?

I try reminding myself in times like these that life mirrors art, and art, life. You don't find yourself in this world, you create yourself. Over and over, detail by detail, you create yourself. And that art, that creation, doesn't fully experience its true value until it meets Death, the great auctioneer.

How to really move with a table through someone's home

In massage school, you might set a table up multiple times a day for practice, but rarely in that process do you ever have to maneuver your table through a narrow hallway or over baby gates. It's a skill that I wish would've been taught (or at least mentioned). But I feel most of the training in school prepares the practitioner for working in a clinic, not in-home massage.

If you're a new massage therapist reading this, practice walking through hallways and awkward areas before going to your first in-home appointment—Hell, step on a Lego or two while you're at it. And remember, it's all in the legs! You have to use your body like a fulcrum by placing the table on your thigh or using your core to pivot. "*PIVOT!*" Practice. Practice. Practice before going into someone's home.

How to actually market yourself

I only remember one tactic they ever raved about in massage school and it went something like this: *just walk up to someone that's talking about their muscular problems in public and offer unsolicited advice and services*. Not only do people not like being eavesdropped on and interrupted, but this scenario rarely happens. Sure, there's probably someone holding this book throwing a tantrum saying *BuT tHaT's HoW I bUiLt My WhOlE pRaCtIcE,* yes, yes, yes, but that doesn't happen to most. Like where are you hanging out at and how good is your hearing?

For real though, the best advice I could give anyone reading this right now is to be as transparent as possible and show your true values in action. People are smart, I know you may not always agree but we're living in an age where everyone is advertising and wants to catch your attention. People have become total pros at ignoring stuff. If they want you, they'll find you. You just have to be easy to find and an obvious fit from the get go. Now, this doesn't mean you just sit in your room and wait for a phone call with good intentions. Get out there and be present in the community—show your values in action. Just please never forget this in your marketing endeavors: people don't know how special you are yet, and they'll never know if you give them a reason to actively ignore you. Be kind, be open, and be proactive in your community.

Oh yeah, and don't pay for marketing. I know how bad that sounds but just don't do it. You do have to pay for a website and business cards and yadda yadda BUT I can count on one hand how many clients I've picked up from paid advertisements for golf club magazines, pharmacy bags, newsletters, banners, or anything else we've got our logo, name, and website printed on. Again, people are awesome at finding what they want and even better at ignoring what they don't want.

That massage should be complemented by other practices

You should combine massage and chiropractic. And massage and acupuncture. And massage and exercise. You should be reaching out to all other modalities and seeing how bodywork can help their patients/clients even more. You should be looking for connection. Looking back, it seems strange that there weren't more fortified relationships with different types of doctors' practices and clinics—we really only invited Massage Envy in to talk to the students. I mean, I get that Massage Envy employs A LOT of new massage therapists and this helps with the placement numbers for the school, but it felt incomplete. It felt like we were just training people to turn them over to the spa life (not a bad thing, but again, not complete).

Biggest mistake massage therapists make

They think minor mastery of a technique and false confidence makes up for being flakey and ill prepared. People can see right through you. If someone feels in their tum tum that you're not totally cool, then it doesn't matter how many different modalities you can do, no one will work with you.

Happiest Memory as an Instructor

But now, for a happy memory. In fact, my happiest, from my days as a massage instructor. I was stressed. I had just handed out the anatomy final to a class and wasn't very confident in the lectures I gave that quarter. I felt like I had set all these people up for failure. So naturally, I was a bit distracted. I sat at the front of the class for a moment and contemplated my inability to teach, and that's when a voice interrupted my thought, "Aren't you gonna say it?"

I always told the class to "put cha books away, get cha pencils out, and put cha thinking caps on" before we took any tests. It was just my way of saying "get ready". I acknowledge her but I'm more caught up in myself and my own thoughts, and I just fumble through it. "radda radda books, pencils, radda caps…"

And that's when everyone in the class pulled out a Batman mask and put it on. Their "thinking caps". The entire class was in on it. I'm a huge Batman nerd and this class knew it. This was their way of saying thank you and it's probably the nicest thing a group of people has ever done for me. And that's a lot, considering this same class threw me a birthday party too. I love and miss you all very much. Thank you for your kindness and I hope you're living the dream.

"ITS NOT WHO WE ARE UNDERNEATH, BUT WHAT WE DO THAT DEFINES US"

I've never met
anyone who was
nearly as Awesome
as you are!
I Love You!
~Toni

You're an amazing teacher
thanks for being awesome!
Stay Awesome! LG

Raf what can I say your
awesome sir I learn a lot
from you - thanks you for
all your hard work and
Dedication to making us
better therapist.
- Jose.

- Raf -
Thank you for making
class fun and enjoyable
You made us laugh and learn
and you cared about each of
us so much will never
forget! - Rox

you were one of my very
favorite instructors of all!
I will miss all your sillyness!
Thank you so much for
everything! Becca

You're definitely one of my favorite
instructors!! I can't begin to tell you how
grateful I am and to have you in my
life. Thanks for your support and... well everything
♡ Hannah I will miss you!!

Thanks for everything
you are an inspiration
Home! LISA

RAF!!!
thanks for
ALL the
fun Facts
& nerding
out with
me! Crystal

Thank you for
everything
- Define :)

Hey Mr. yor
are an amazing
human being!
you have that
teaching style
that reaches
everyone with
a mathwide
open! I really
liked the way
you taught us
Anatomy you
made it one of
my fav. sub!
Thanks! :)
- Daniel ♥
COOL
STUFF

60

Raf ♡
I will never
forget you...
Your kind, awesome,
positive energy was
a pleasure to be around!
You are such a beautiful
human being.
Thank you
♥♥♥

Raf, you teaching techniques
were amazing, teaching me as I
went through everything you
didn't understand my knowledge
and will use so many
beautiful things from you ♡
gosh!"

Hallmark

Bonus memory!

That time I straight up 'pwned' an entire class with my 3rd grade math skills. But not like "Ben Shapiro 'destroys' a crowd", but more like Lord Frieza pwning the entire planet Vegeta and all the Saiyans on it (it's totally okay if you didn't understand that last sentence, but welcome to my mind 😊).

So, I used to lead a pathology course when I worked for the massage school. On this day we were going over the cardiovascular system and at one point started talking about the heart. I like fun facts and laid this little treat down, "the heart pumps roughly five to seven liters a minute." And a student, with a most offended tone, responds with, "but our anatomy teacher told us the heart pumps 5 to 7 **quarts** per minute, not liters."

So I respond with, "Quarts and liters are basically the same size, so don't sweat it."

AND THEN TOTAL CHAOS ERRUPTED LIKE NO OTHER. I had people yelling and making poopy faces at me— you know that face. Just imagine a baby's face when pooping and compare it to any angry adult, it's… hilariously accurate. One guy even tried comparing 2.5-liter soda bottles (which he thought were a representation of a single liter) to milk gallons in order to convince me that quarts are way smaller than liters.

Now, if you're reading and thinking, "*Oh you idiot. You pathetic, massive, uncensored man-child…do ye not know anything… ANYTHING AT ALL? Quarts and liters…they're different…right?*" You're not wrong, .95 liters is roughly equal to a quart. As in, a liter is 95% the same size as a quart. AS IN, basically, for our purposes, they're the same size, so don't sweat it.

Okay, okay, okay just put the book down and google it then. I know you don't believe me. Wait never mind, I'll save you the hassle with a screen shot. BAM! Next page.

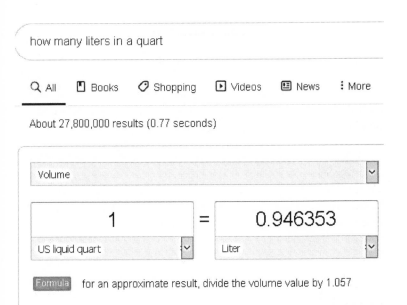

how many liters in a quart

Q All   📖 Books   🧭 Shopping   ▶️ Videos   📰 News   ⋮ More

About 27,800,000 results (0.77 seconds)

Volume

| 1 | = | 0.946353 |

US liquid quart | Liter

Formula for an approximate result, divide the volume value by 1.057

I can't really say there's any feeling like it; having 30+ people argue with you only to tell them to pull out their smart phones and look it up themselves. I still think back on how the smug, poopy diaper filled faces turned to soured embarrassment upon realizing their mistake. That confidence in numbers turning to shame of the masses. That vehemence turned to trepidation. So sweet. (Let this be a lesson. Feeling right and feeling angry can feel identical. Just because you feel right doesn't make you right.)

The mood quickly reset to a jovial atmosphere, at least they could laugh at themselves—I know I was laughing at them. NOW, TO THEIR DEFENSE, it is a running joke in the massage world that our practitioners are the absolute worst at math. We convey table height by the rungs on the legs of the table, and per class I'd have to come by and count everyone's rungs to make sure they were even on all four legs— and without exaggeration at least one person every class counted wrong. We were counting no higher than six each time and that's if you're taller...so...yeah...I guess that makes me the bully here, huh? Picking on poor, defenseless American adults that can't count or google stuff—I'm a monster! Who the hell do I think I am?

deep inhale through the nostrils *You smell that kids? That's an American education...Stings the nostrils...60% of the time, it works every time...* (name that movie reference and get a FREE high five. Plus, once you're done reading it as Brian Fantana, try rereading it with Stan's voice from 'American Dad'. You're welcome.)

III

Unstoppable Force
V. Immovable Object

LMT's V. DPT's:

Why Are They Such Dicks to Us?

On multiple occasions, I've had to deal with grumpy physical therapists (side rant – totally was marketing at a gym once and had a physical therapist walk past me and say, "you know that stuff doesn't work, right?" I replied, "Oh, okay." And gave her smile. She proceeded to scream and throw a tantrum as she walked away, "It doesn't! *It dooooesn't!*" It was like something out of a horror movie. And of course, she had to keep eye contact the entire time and I swear I heard a Joker type laugh as she disappeared into the locker rooms. I still have nightmares about her). I really thought for a while that I just had a poor attitude I was unaware of towards doctors of physical therapy(DPTs), but then I was at a continuing education course with other licensed massage therapists (LMT's) and everyone in the class mentioned that they consistently had run ins with them as well. So, it got me thinkin'…

Maybe the clash rests in the fact that our fields overlap? Massage and physical therapists both perform manual therapies on the body, and both have insight into movements/exercises that will correct posture and help you move better. But where the big differences lie are in the time spent with each client/patient (no other type of practitioner palpates the body more than a massage therapist does), the ability to diagnose (LMTs can't do this. We may do an assessment for our own purposes, but we can't officially declare a diagnosis), and amount of education (they clearly have more). But that doesn't fully explain why they're such cranky assholes.

Well, LMT's are not totally blameless in this. As we've discussed in chapters prior, massage therapists can have a knack for being flakey and unreliable. Not only that, some massage therapists have performed outside of their scope of practice in the past and lost us credibility with other fields. The worst one I heard was that some gal was diagnosing her clients with herniated discs because she could 'feel' them in their spine. I'm not saying she isn't feeling something, but I am saying it's not a herniated disc. And even if she did intuitively know somehow like a true gangsta shaman, it's just not something you say at that level of training. You might suggest they see a doctor that you trust for confirmation if you really feel like somethings wrong, but just laying it out there like that is thoroughly not recommended.

I even worked with instructors that didn't truly understand what our scope of practice was. I worked with an instructor that would regularly psychoanalyze people and their childhoods and try to give advice on things WAY outside of her scope. Just not cool, man. (Probably still cooler than the massage instructor I worked with who had zero experience all together. He had never held a professional massage gig outside of his teaching position. Just how…?)

But hell, how can I hold it against DPT's? It's not like massage therapists even get along with each other. So many LMT's act threatened when around other practitioners. I can't tell you how many times I've had to deal with other whiny bodyworkers and their insecurities—I was even uninvited to an event once because the other person working the event couldn't handle it. So, I can't entirely blame physical therapists for almost looking at us like their annoying little siblings. But that still doesn't give them a pass to be rude. Manners maketh man.

(Quick side story – When my wife and I started our business, we made many attempts to connect with professionals in other fields, such as physical therapists and chiropractors. So, one day I find myself at a physical therapy office and am speaking with a doctor—but I'm the only one talking. She just stared at me and mumbled back what I assumed were answers, but it sounded like she was just repeating what I was saying in a low, sinister whisper until I just left. Brilliant really; it was a super effective tactic that got me to leave fast.

Okay, okay, another quick side story – I was working a marketing event and there were a couple of DPT's there as well. At one point as I'm giving massage, I look over and this guy is shaking his head while staring at me with disgust in his eyes. I asked him if there was anything I could help him out with and he just got up and left. I dunno…I just hope the whole "staring into my soul as they disappear" thing doesn't keep up. Like, is this a course they're all required to take in school or something? Creep level 100. *Find someone who looks at you, the same way this physical therapist looks at Raf.)*

In fact, I really hope our fields can start to work together more. Often, I hear the same complaint from clients about their physical therapy sessions, "the short, manual therapy treatment relieved a lot of pain, but then they sat me down to do exercises and I didn't see the doctor again." I've had some clients just learn (then forget) the exercises and start getting massage instead. But I also think these patients/clients never really got the point to begin with: movement is key. It may be bothersome, but it's the best way to get you moving again. Without it, you're not going to make the progress that you want. There are tools to help you along the way, but you have to put in that work. But with all this in mind, my question is this: if we know that the client/patient is feeling overlooked, they don't feel like they're progressing, they like the manual work, don't fully understand movement, and we have all the tools to help, then why can't we change? Why don't our practices work more closely? Why does it have to be one or the other? Sure, some of it probably has to be insurance related, but why can't we play zone defense on this? Of course, the doctor is seeing multiple patients at once. Of course, your exercises are important. But of course, the client having time spent with a professional and feeling heard is just as important.

So, what do you say…*friends*?

Work WITH Chiropractors, Not FOR Chiropractors

Okay, so big disclaimer, working for a chiropractor is not a bad thing. There's plenty of amazing talent out there that you should work for. But understand, I've met plenty of cheapskates and crackpots in my years too. It's actually really easy to tell the difference between a good and bad chiropractor. Here it is: if they are thorough, listen to you, take their time, don't ask you for thousands of dollars up front for treatments, and don't put you a schedule for 45 times a week as they charge your insurance for every code possible, then they're probably good people. But I've worked for "bad" chiropractors before; the kind of people that look like the word 'narcissist'.

I was once sent to "business academy" for chiropractors in order to receive training in getting new patients to buy expensive wellness plans. I was going to be the guy that convinced you spending thousands of dollars on adjustments was a much better idea then just coming in and paying when you needed it. It was a costly program (like 5 digits kind of cost) that revolved around sitting in a room for a weekend and filling out a packet (think like 3rd grade classwork packet kind of packet) that would supposedly train you to be able to sell to anyone under any conditions. You know, every capitalist's dream class. Basically, these people were selling a stack of papers for thousands of dollars and getting away with it. (ALSO! BTW! This company totally taught chiropractors to invest in the smallest rooms possible for the massage therapist employees because it was cheaper, and you actually DO want turnover in this field. Their words not mine. It revolves around the insecurity that someone whose been around for years may leave and take a large portion of patients with them. Plus, there's always new talent coming out looking for any entry level positions. Who cares if you use and abuse then hire someone new? Well, Raf does. At the last clinic I worked for, the boss asked me to shred some papers in my downtime. As I made my way through my task, I counted 26 other massage therapists that had been hired and fired/quit within the year prior to that. That's the kind of potential turn over I'm talking about.)

Now, this was at a time when I was obsessed with finding information on the web. I still believe you can literally find anything, for free, if it's been presented to the public in anyway. *You just have to know where to look.* *cracks knuckles and just simply googles it* And with a little bit of searching, I did find the packet the business academy sold us. BUT my search didn't bring me to the business academies site or its cashed files, but rather to the Church of Scientology. The freaking Church of Scientology! Yes, the packet that cost thousands of dollars and contained information that we would push to our patients, was written by L. Ron Hubbard and was being disguised as a business tutorial for beginning chiropractors and their staff.

What in the actual fuck? I don't care for Scientology and I don't care for being lied to.

Now, the chiro I worked for wasn't aware of this until I made my discovery. So, I couldn't blame the guy…at first. After I came forth with this info, he demoted me and sent someone else to academy instead. And he didn't even do that in a classy way, I was made aware of my demotion during a staff meeting while he was congratulating my replacement on her promotion. Grade "A" asshole.

I just have to add, for perspective on the man, this was the guy who tried to connect an HDMI cable to his ethernet cable to get HD internet. I told him it doesn't work like that, so he had me call the IT guy, who then said, "Ugh…I already told him it doesn't work like that. Put him on."

And this is the same guy who was traveling to a conference with my wife. Before they departed for home, he boastfully claimed that he put the exact amount of gas in the car to get to his doorstep (don't let your car run out of gas, it's bad for it). He ran out of gas like halfway, got towed to nearest gas station. WHERE HE REPEATED THE SAME THING. Didn't even fill the tank up because of how much confidence he had in his math skills. I didn't let my wife drive with him after that.

THIS IS THE SAME GUY that would randomly mention stuff after meetings like, "Did you know animals are gay too. It acts as a natural population control? They can instinctually feel when the herd is too big and voluntarily become homosexual, just like humans." *Uhhh…? Da fuck…?*

THIS IS THE SAAAAAAAME GUUUUUUY who would only play "Paradise" by Coldplay in the lobby. Just that **one** song over and over again. "Para, para, paradise. Para, para, paradise." Needless to say, he had an incredibly high turnover rate with the front desk personnel.

THIS IS THE SAAAAAAAAAAAAME GUUUUUUUUY who would encourage his employees to put down extra codes so they could bill the insurance company more. There're rules to this kind of stuff and breaking those rules is considered insurance fraud. Don't listen to morons that encourage insurance fraud, no matter how much 'logic' they seem to present with.

THIS IS THE SAAAAAAAAAAAAAAAAAAAAAAME GUUUUUUUUUUUY who almost fired me and my wife because we were volunteering our massage skills to retired service members. He brought up some bullshit about a competition clause and threatened to relieve us of our jobs if we didn't quit volunteering our time to veterans.

The moral of the story(ies) being, as a separate entity, I never have to worry about this happening or being a part of my regular day. Our entire relationship revolves around the client's health and that's where the line is drawn. There's a balance in power dynamic when you work more as equals. If I work for a chiro and don't like how they operate, then I'm out of a job. But if I have my own clients, then I get to act as a filter before recommending any other professionals. Approval is gained when other practitioners demonstrate that they have the same values and attention to detail that I do.

But again, if you work for a talented, honest doctor, then you don't have to worry about this.

BE-TEE-DOUBLE U! Big thanks to Dr. Danielle Miller, Dr. Justin Gehling, Dr. Oryan Salberg, and Dr.'s Tiffany and Jerome Longoria—you've all been amazing, and it's been a pleasure to work with you. Keep up the awesome, honest work. I love you all.

How Do I Feel About Acupuncturists?

I love 'em. I don't think I've ever met an acupuncturist I didn't like. Big shout out to Jennifer Roseman and Katie Reed for your guidance and friendship.

Massage therapists are often taught 'acupressure' which is basically acupuncture without the needles. Same points but held with the fingers instead. No puncture, just pressure. Although it can be useful, if you're looking for traditional Chinese medicine (TCM), then I say you should go all the way. There's really no substituting what a talented acupuncturist can do, but if you're new to TCM and are interested in being introduced, asking your massage therapist might be a good place to start.

Also, much like with chiropractors or any other professionals, I still recommend working 'with' instead of 'for' but do what works for you. I've met some acupuncturist that want massage therapy involved with their patients and clients, but don't want to do it themselves (it can be taxing). Which can make for a potentially great symbiotic relationship.

Owning a Business V. Working for a Business

Both are hard and although I'm going to bring up complaints about being an employee instead of the employer, this chapter isn't about choosing one or the other, but rather, why I decided to take the route that I took. I think the attractiveness of being my own boss can be summed up into this: being solely responsible for how I use my time and energy, to be most effective. Now, obviously, you can have this as an employee (and especially as a contractor), but there were plenty of times as an employee that I had the thought of _we could be way more successful if we just changed_ [blank] but [blank] was always going to be a part of the job. An example:

Most staff meetings are a waste of time and convey an amazing amount of disrespect to the staff. Although these meetings may have wholesome intent, they tend to waste everyone's time except for two: 1) the boss who thinks announcing something makes it official and puts it into motion (think Michael Scott from The Office, "I… declare… bankruptcy!" "I just wanted you to know, you can't just say the word 'bankruptcy' and expect anything to happen." "I didn't say it; I declared it."). This is normally void of any real instructions and rarely accounts for when things don't go as 'planned'. And 2) the person that thinks these meetings are called specifically for them to have a platform to tell their personal stories from the week prior (just write a book for crying out loud 😊). Their stories normally go something like this when speaking of an interaction they had, "Then I was like _ugh._ And they were like _mmhmm._ And so, I was like _*eye roll*_ and they were like _uh-huh._ So, I was like _uh-uh no way._ And they were like _blah de freaking blah blah blah_" And they never actually come to a conclusion to their story. Just a circle story with no end. Waste. Of. Time. In an age where email and conference video has been fully integrated into our lives, there's no excuse as to why most meetings can't be digital and save everyone the hassle of showing up to a meeting. Which leads me to my next point.

Why are staff meetings always scheduled at the most awkward times? Either you come in earlier, you come in on a day off, or come in to go home to come back for a later shift. I asked this to my previous employer, and he gave me the answer of, "It's just always been that way." Where's that capitalist's innovation I'm always hearing so much about? This is just coasting until you hit hard waters. But it's also something you can't control unless you're the captain. So, I have to wonder what other possible avenues there could be.

Well, if these meetings had some organization and were actually about brainstorming and input, then I'd be all for them. But even then, most brainstorming sessions beyond three people tend to start excluding others in the group. It comes down to the simple system of a chain of command. A small group reporting to higher ups on what needs to change, finding solutions to the problem, and then bringing it even higher up. There's this impression that a group of people shouting what they want or even a group of people being told what they want has effectiveness, but there's just one problem: there's no one in the middle of that process that's sincerely trying to figure out the steps in the system that need to change. It normally comes down to receiving complaints then either nothing changes, or you have big changes that don't make sense, followed by mass exodus.

Being my own boss allows me to change this part of the equation. The meetings with my wife and I (she owns the company with me) are action packed and solution based. Step by step instructions and dates are set. You should end an effective meeting with a list that details a plan for success—this must include deadlines and who's accountable for what. If you don't have this, then what progress can you plan to make? And if you're not making progress, then what was the point of the damn meeting?

75

Okay, side rant – Power dynamics and the Game of Thrones mentality in the workplace

Is just something I can't stand. I do not care that you have more 'seniority' because you've been here the longest and made the least impact. Growing up I was introduced to martials arts and more so appreciate their form of seniority—it's not about how long you've been somewhere, but rather about your accomplishments. When I was in the process of moving up the ranks at the massage school, it was common to hear that someone was 'next in line' to fill the coveted full-time instructor position, whenever it became available. So many people relied on their time spent at the company rather than skill learned. Everyone's just waiting around to be king.

Double side rant – The parking lot dilemma

It seems like at every job there's at least one person that doesn't understand the spot directly in front of the clinic/ spa/ school/ office isn't for them, but rather the customers and guests. And they always take great offense when you tell them to literally park anywhere else in the parking lot. A sea of parking spaces to choose from and they want the one right up front. I once worked with a gal who was told to not park in front of the office, so she went next door, and they said the same thing. BUT THEN! There was, like, this parking war with the business on the other side. Because wouldn't you know it, they also had a gal who didn't understand how parking lots worked. So, these two battled it out like parking gladiators—none were victorious.

We all know this person, by the way. We all have one of these in our lives. They have to park as close as possible to the entrance, they go into cashier's lane with the light OFF and ask if they're still open, they don't return their grocery carts to the coral, they litter, they do a partial stop at stop signs, don't use their blinker when changing lanes or turning, they take an inappropriate amount of selfies, they leave like a little dribble of milk in the carton instead of just finishing it, and they do the same to the cereal…that person. I don't want to work with that person. I don't even want to remotely deal with that person. Why are there so many of them? Like some horrible Attack of the Clones remake.

T-T-TRIPLE SIDE RANT?!

Having a schedule that makes sense to me is important. As nonsensical as it might sound, having a flexible schedule is the kind that makes sense. I have set hours on our website, but my team and I can always work outside or change those hours and choose what works best for client and therapist. "Notice that the stiffest tree is most easily cracked, while the bamboo or willow survives by bending with the wind." –Bruce Lee

I remember working at a clinic and was tasked with being the lead therapist. I got to do the trainings every week while relaying requests from the team members—I played telephone with management, basically. Because of this, I had Saturdays off and Sundays the clinic was closed. It didn't take long before the crew said this was unfair and asked that we share the Saturdays; an alternating schedule. Although it didn't seem right to me, I guess it was fair, so I agreed. Although I was bummed about the change, I figured it was best for team morale and what a 'good leader' should do. But it was the looks on their faces when the schedule came out and everyone realized they weren't getting ALL Saturdays off, but rather one Saturday every two months (because that's how math works), that admittedly put a smile on my face. It was like one of those movie scenes where the bank robbers just figured out if they start killing each other than they can get bigger shares of the loot.

Running my own business has allowed me to work with a schedule independent of other workers and because of our business model, any of our workers can change theirs without impact to me. Sure, there's still some consistency needed, and you won't always enjoy the long days, but having the power to alter your schedule can severely influence how you view your work and what kind of attitude you bring to it. Regarding my story at the beginning of the chapter, what if no one had to come in on Saturday and all those hours were made up elsewhere? What if Saturdays had been made longer for a set few (the day was only three hours long) and less people were on staff that day? What if? What if? I can now ask the "what if" question with confidence that I can do something about it. When working for someone, it's really their call and on their time.

Moreover, having a schedule that you control makes a big difference if the client or practitioner becomes ill. When you're working in a clinic with a team, often it's made out to sound like you have others there to cover for you if you're sick, which we all know is a hassle in itself. You wake up with a fever and jet engine propelled diarrhea only to jump through all the hoops of calling everyone that's got the day off so they can tell you they already have plans, then you call the boss and tell them no one can cover for you and you're not coming in, so they make a policy about how you can't be sick anymore. *PrObLeM sOlVeD!*

I've never run into issues calling clients directly and rescheduling them. The only people that have ever made a big deal out of being sick are managers (which by the way, most managers you see at these clinics, spas and even schools have ZERO massage experience. The owners somehow have even less.). There's also more you can do to make it up to the client if they are offended you're sick OR you can easily refer that person to someone else (if they're really that offended that you're sick).

I did work for a guy who came up with a system of "so-and-so will be on-call for this shift" and so on and so on, which makes sense on paper but is easily abused—by both employer and employee. I really don't mind an on-call system when its used properly. Especially when you're compensated well, and your time is used wisely. But if you had Friday or Saturday night off, you could bet someone would call out for some kind of personal event, so you would have 'no choice' (you always have a choice) but to drop what you were doing and fill in for this person. No joke, I had someone tell me they were "going to be sick tomorrow", right after they told me about a concert they wanted to go to that night.

And of course, the employer, the same guy that suggested an on-call system cut all our pay because he took one too many vacations that year (it was common for him to cut our pay mid-vacation). So, people quit. And because of this draconian on-call policy, you were expected to fill in for extra hours for 75% of the pay.

And I can hear it already, "*DaMn MiLllEnIaLs! I mAdE 10 cEnTs A—*" blah blah blah. I currently make about $75 an hour, I normally made $15/hr with this guy and he eventually cut me to $11.25—it doesn't take some magical boomer genius or work ethic to figure out which one is total bologna and a waste of time. Besides, you don't last as long as I have in this field by abusing your body and not giving your tools ample rest.

Recovering from an injury costs WAY more than just treating your body with respect and taking breaks. Yes, yes, you have to push yourself and work hard, but that doesn't mean you have to be a sucker. And if someone who's profiting off your hard work doesn't like when you're not acting like a sucker, you just say to them what my favorite Spider-man said to the crass wrestling promoter who shorted him, "*I missed the part where that's my problem.*"

Why I Left the Spa Life

Before I get started into this chapter, I have to say, big corporate massage chains, as a whole, get too much flak. Yes, it doesn't make any sense that their business models still exists and yes, we've all heard some kind of horror story from our massage therapist about them, but those places can really be tools to sharpen your skills (especially in the beginning) if you just let them be. The spa life in a big chain massage company was my intro to the field. It was unforgiving and did not pay well but it taught me to think under pressure, control my attitude, and how to produce power in a session without wasting it. If you can make it in one of the big corporate chains, you can make it anywhere as a massage therapist. And I think that should be cherished. Plus, probably once a week I gain a client from these big companies simply because we don't charge for a membership. Especially one that won't let you redeem the massages you purchased at the start of the new year.

I appreciate these big companies and congratulate them on their success; I just don't think they're the type of place I would spend my whole career. So, let's get into it—why I left. There were plenty of small things that got under my skin that I shouldn't have let. I worked for one spa that wouldn't call me 'Raf' (my full name is Erik Rafael King, but I've gone by Raf my whole life.) because "the computer system wouldn't let them change people's names" *overly exaggerated shrug*. Keeping in mind, I worked with guys named Oliver, Salvador, and Ryan that went by the names, in and out of the system, as Ollie, Sal, and Dalu. Da-freaking-lu. (BTW, I totally don't hold anything against these guys. I got along with all of them and one even came to work for me for a short while. It's just the only person I've met who had a problem with me not going by Erik, was my super racist 2nd grade teacher. She really set the bar for everyone that preferred I go by 'Erik' instead of 'Raf'.) For you see, many people misunderstand why lying is so bad. It's not just because your bending the truth. But it's because you're bending the truth with the understanding that the person you're lying to is dumb enough to believe you. It's like compounding insults without even trying. We'll come back to this in a moment, though. But yes, once I called them out about it, they admitted that they found my name to be just "too weird", and people didn't "get it". Like it's some kind of fucking joke or something?

Other small things that have happened while I was working at a certain big chain spa include but are not limited to:

We could only bring clear bags into work. This was their way of trying to deter theft. Someone got away with table warmers, blankets, pillows, sheets and headrests and they thought clear bags would help. How does one even fit an entire table warmer into their purse? Maybe under their shirt?

They fired someone for not showing up for their shift. They were in a diabetic coma.

They threaten to fire someone for pointing out to the staff that they didn't have to clean the clinic without pay (they went by a pay-per-session type of system. Meaning, if you weren't massaging, then you weren't being paid), it was even advertised on their website as such. She literally printed off pages from their website, posted them in the breakroom, and she was met with near termination.

They threaten to fire people for talking about movies they didn't like—now okay, this one is understandable and probably shouldn't make the list. Some movies can be a bit extreme and inappropriate. But I think it was more the rationale that went into it and how it was handled that bothered me. Instead of just asking us to change the subject in that moment, the manager waited till there was a staff meeting to make personal attacks in front of people and explain her thought process as, "If I can't fathom switching subjects from movies to massage that fast, then neither can you". That same lady called me a "pompous asshole" when she thought I wasn't listening.

She was aggressive, just not confrontational. You know? One of those people who has to be seen publicly doing the 'right' thing but is an utter piece of shit privately.

As a 225-pound male (at the time), they gave me women's medium sized shirts then threaten to fire me because if my pants ever slid down from being hiked up to my nipples, you might see the tops of my underwear or bottom on my undershirt. There was a charge for exchanging shirts and acquiring new ones. So why didn't I just *buy* extra shirts, damnit? I think Macklemore best explains this as getting "swindled and pimped… getting tricked by a business". And I ain't about dat life, yo.

And they would do this awful thing that really made my life harder (btw, if you're a clinic that does this, I would strongly recommend that you stop doing this. It creates more problems than it solves): when a client would call in, they would ask, "would you like a male or female massage therapist?" For most new people calling in to schedule a massage, they haven't thought about it. And, AND, it really doesn't matter IF it doesn't really matter to you. If you do have a preference, then you know to ask in the first place. And people are entitled to ask, for sure— you don't even need to say why. But asking the client this when they haven't given it any thought, normally leads one way, to the female massage therapist. Why? I suspect one of two reasons: 1) Because it kind of makes sense. Your brain categorizes and generalizes, and generally speaking, women seem to be more nurturing than men (I mean, they only produce life and carry babies and then feed those babies with their bodies…so yeah, men come in a close second) even if we've encountered people who embody the opposite traits. I grew up without a mother and was raised by a very nurturing father. But that doesn't make me see all men differently, and when making a snap decision, you may just go with that part of the brain that generalizes and leads you to what you think is more nurturing. And 2) it introduces the idea of sex into a practice that earnestly tries to separate itself from such a topic. Massage therapy has had a long history of being involved with prostitution and human trafficking, but modern-day massage has really pushed to separate itself from such practices and bring revived credibility to bodywork. Any good person doesn't seek massage for sexual purposes, only creeps do that. Asking someone about a preference that normally relates to sex reframes the conversation and forces them to ask an odd question, *"do I wanna be 'rubbed down' by a man or a woman?"* Why don't we just ask if they prefer their massage therapist to be straight or gay? —I mean, since we're already discussing their genitalia and asking their preference. Or maybe we ask about breast size and skin color while we're at it? Let's just really tailor the whole experience. Why don't we ask any of these things as they're scheduling, because it doesn't matter and neither does the gender of your massage therapist. Easy fix: after you've asked what time and day they want their massage at, read a list of the therapists' names. You can even put the least booked person in front when you read the list.

But…bum bum bummmm…why I *really* left the big soulless corporate spa life. So, there are some pretty standard forms you sign when you start working at a company. They're obvious and you normally have someone sit down and go over it with you. You sign and review them and maybe even get a copy. The point being, a lot of these agreements are taken care of at the start and are transparent. A spa I worked for decided to hand out some legal forms during a staff meeting and tried making them sound like no big deal. "Just sign this and get it back to me, ASAP". I clearly remember the admin rushing everyone to get their signatures down and turn them back in. That, of course, triggered the opposite response. The more we read the more uncomfortable we became. Remember earlier when I had that whole rant about lying? Yeeeeeah… so not only did they assume we'd sign and hand it back, they then assumed we wouldn't question why they would want to keep this a secret. The form they wanted us to sign was a standard agreement that would require you to seek mediation before suing the company. But the company reserved the right to take 364 days to bring any attention to your claim, they got to choose the location, the mediator, and could be in mediation for up to a year. So basically, it could take almost two years before legal action could be taken. Again, this is standard, you've probably signed something like this in the past. But it looks shady when someone tries to slip this in and pull a fast one on you. It looks like the company is knee deep in something and looking for a raft (haha that sounds like 'Raf', like my name. Welcome to the childhood joke I heard on repeat, over and over again.).

When people refused to sign, they started a mass firing process. I was a part of that group. Not much time would pass before I started reading about lawsuit after lawsuit involving this big massage chain. Last I checked, there are over 400 sexual assault cases brought against them (and by "them" I mean dozens of independently owned franchises under one name. Which is important to differentiate, because even though I'm throwing a lot of general shade towards an entire company and 'the spa life' in this chapter, the truth is every clinic should be judged individually and should be divorced from the deeds of their sister establishments). And this doesn't even include the numerous cases related to continually charging for memberships after they were cancelled and price hikes. This certain big chain massage company was sued for continuing to charge people for a membership that they cancelled. They also try (even still as this book is being written) enforcing that their clients can't bring forth any legal claims against them or any of their affiliates. Meaning, you may be a loyal customer, but they have no loyalty to you. They want you silent. They encouraged those 400 sexual assault victims to stay quiet with their agreement. This was taken from their website:

"AT NO TIME SHALL YOU HAVE A RIGHT TO, NOR SHALL YOU, ASSERT OR BRING ANY CLAIM, DEMAND, OR LEGAL ACTION AGAINST MEF OR ANY OF ITS AFFILIATES RELATING TO YOUR MEMBERSHIP OR WELLNESS AGREEMENT OR THE SERVICES PROVIDED UNDER THE AGREEMENT."

Let me clear a little of that up for you, "At no time shall you have a right to…bring any…legal action against MEF or its affiliates relating to…the services provided." Or in other words, you can't sue them for what your massage therapist did to you—it's all part of the 'services provided'. Even if it is heinous, that's just part of it. That's the spin they've put on it and its disgusting.

I read some details about a few of the cases—I didn't make it far. I like the occasional horror flick, but this was truly the stuff of nightmares. I'm glad to not be affiliated with any part of them anymore.

I'm not very good at writing inspiring types of work, so I'll leave it the words of the great Frank Herbert. If anyone from the 400, or anyone that should speak up like the 400 did, is reading this, I have this to leave with you: "I must not fear. Fear is the mind-killer. Fear is the little-death that brings total obliteration. I will face my fear. I will permit it to pass over me and through me. And when it has gone past I will turn the inner eye to see its path. Where the fear has gone there will be nothing. Only I will remain." —Frank Herbert, Dune

Why I Left the Massage School

I left my instructor's position from the massage school for a lot of reasons, but there's one that seems to stick out to me. I hope the reader can understand that this is my side of it. I'm sure *she* would have another story to tell.

I dated a coworker when I was instructing at the school. She was in another department and we typically kept everything professional. Most students couldn't tell there was anything between us. That was until we broke up. She didn't take it very well and started harassing me at work. Now, I don't like to use that word lightly, particularly because some individuals have lived through far worse, but she did, on a daily basis, in front of other staff and students, sing and laugh about my genitals. So, it wasn't the worst, BUT it was a terrible combination: an entire staff turning a blind eye and a person growing more confident in their endeavors. So, of course, it did get worse. I tried to handle it as a gentleman, but with no obvious effect. It wasn't until my conversation with a student that the line was finally drawn.

I had a student come to me because in class, as everyone was practicing massage, he had an extreme emotional response to the work. "I can see my dead wife every time I close my eyes." His words still haunt me. Even to this day this thought gives me shivers. He goes on to mention how her social media accounts had been hacked and he was receiving messages from those accounts. He needed consoling; he needed a friend. What he didn't need was to think that my ex was actually making fun of *his* genitals and telling *him* he deserved everything that was happening to him. His face, I remember that face of pain. Reeling in embarrassment— it took something from me, seeing a man in that kind of pain. It was after that that I went to management to figure out a solution. Can you guess the response of not only my manager, but her manager, and our managers' manager? It's all the same, like they rehearsed it together or something: "We talked to her, and she doesn't know what you're talking about, at all. Sorry. There's nothing we can do."

None of my fellow instructors would say anything but I eventually convinced some of my TA's to testify on my behalf and confirm her behavior. It was by no means easy and had zero fucking impact.

Weeks went by, then the director of the school called me into his office one day. Asked me to sit down and be quiet. He picked up the phone, dialed a line, and put it on speaker. The head of the HR department answered, and he asked her about my case. "Listen, this is crazy and even with all those testimonies he brought to you, this won't hold up. Who's ever heard of a man being sexually harassed by a woman, anyway? I'm sorry, but there's nothing we're going to do about this." (Remember kids, the human resources department is there to protect the company, not you. Because corporations are people now, but not people that have to follow the law, just people that are protected by it.) He thanked her and hung up the phone. "You see what I'm dealing with here? I'm sorry, but my hands are tied."

It was like being hit with a fucking cinderblock. I don't know how I found the words, hell, maybe they found me, "Thank you, I know you're doing everything that you can. But I don't feel comfortable representing myself anymore, and I'm going to find representation for this matter." Although my words came out clear and concise, my body is shaking at this point. I can feel my chest starting to buzz. *Why can't I breathe?! I need to leave.* I'm prone to panic attacks and I know ones about to hit big.

"Wait, wait, wait, wait, wait. I'll have this taken care of by tomorrow."

I didn't know what that meant at the time and didn't care. I loved this place, I loved my work, and I looked to my colleagues as if they were my heroes. All that died that day. Part of me always knew I wasn't part of the team—hell, like there ever really was a team. Just a group of people fooled into getting along.

The next day I came into work and my ex had been fired. The email said, "she's moved on to brighter opportunities" and mentioned she had quit. Which was a lie. And exactly what I *didn't* want to happen. I just wanted her to stop. She was hurt and took a dark path, I know, but she didn't deserve this. It hurts knowing she lost her income. It hurts knowing people came up to me afterwards and told me they never liked her—that feeling of knowing that no one around me was genuine in their speech or actions, like a bunch of two-faced snakes. All these people said they hadn't seen anything and all tucked tail when I needed them. It didn't feel like a victory at all. We both lost. She didn't have the most valuable thing you could have in this society, and I hated everyone. All my heroes look like sloppy losers now.

I didn't last much longer after that. New management stepped in a few months later and I stepped out. My dad started having heart problems and I needed to take time off to spend with him. I didn't communicate it well enough, that's on me, but I saw their faces when they had a chance to force me out instead of waiting for me to leave—the excitement that danced in their eyes and my disgust that echoed. Part of me didn't want to communicate it better, my dad's heart. Part of me wanted the excuse to finally leave. I was tired. Towards the end I was getting into the office at 8:30am and leaving around 11:00pm. Either way, I'm happy to be gone and last I heard they drove that place into the ground without me; the dojo is no longer. I don't think I'll ever go back to instructing at a school—that part of my life is over. There's something about institutions that drive me crazy now. I like to think I left instructing to be reluctantly pulled back in, but the truth is I've had several offers over the past few years and they all gave me the same feeling deep in my gut. I know it sounds pathetic, but I still have nightmares from that place. It still wakes me up in the middle of the night. It's gotten better though; my wife says I no longer chatter my teeth in my sleep (bless her soul for not smothering me. I love you baybuh!).

Side Rant Time!

Another big reason I left was the obvious double standard in the school. Unfortunately, it seemed like race and gender played huge roles in how people were treated. Being white or a woman or both, significantly increased your chances of flying under the radar. For example, we had a light skinned girl in the program who went into the restroom, phoned a friend that she'd be leaving the drugs in the 2nd stall's trashcan and she could leave the money there. We know this because a staff member was in the first stall and overheard the whole thing. She collected the bag of pills and reported it to the director and police department. Oh, oh, let's play 'guess the outcome'. Nothing happened. Technically, the school was renting one level of the complex and wasn't responsible for anything outside of their front door, which is where the restrooms were located. And PD said there wasn't any *actual* exchange of money and drugs, so there was nothing they could do either. Life just went on with the knowledge that she failed miserably at a drug deal. Like seriously, she just showed up the next day and everyone knew, but just had to go about their day as usual.

I also remember a white guy, former military, making his hand into the shape of a gun and pretending to shoot classmates as they set up tables. Nothing happened there either. In fact, he was real chummy with all the instructors and staff.

But now let's draw our attention to man with dark skin. He came into class one day, obviously not feeling well. When a fellow classmate asked him what was wrong, he responded with, "I had a terrible nightmare last night, I dreamt I blew up our graduation." He was immediately reported and kicked out of school (no PD called). They labeled him a sociopath who was looking for approval from classmates to commit mass murder. Neither the director nor education manager were trained psychologist who could make that call. Now, am I defending him? It certainly sounds like I am, but no. Rather, I feel situations like these could have been handled way better and with more consistency. He was kicked out of school because of perceived intent and something he said, what about the other two people? What about the person who intended to sell narcotics on campus? Or the guy who 'joked' about a shooting spree? Why weren't the police called for this incident as well? I'm ashamed I didn't stand up more for people. I'm ashamed of my inaction. But I was a scared boy who just wanted to keep his 'high paying', steady job. I was looking for security in the eighth circle of hell.

Double Side Rant

Another shady practice they indulged in was bringing individuals with felonies on their records into the program without telling them that their felony disqualified them from begin licensed after graduation. Basically, they would pursue people trying to change their lives for the better, leave out the part where they can't make a living from it, and then trick them into thousands of dollars of debt. I can't tell you how many amazing people I met that fell into this category—it was heart breaking to see. I believe people can change; I truly do. Yes, when you make a mistake you must pay the price, but that doesn't mean you should have pay again and again. ESPECIALLY when you're trying to make such a positive change in your life.

This wasn't the only kind of person they ripped off either. It was common to recruit students that had no high school education— some didn't even know how to read. All for the sake of keeping "their numbers" high enough. But in the end, I believe it's what lead to their own collapse.

Triple Side Rant

Probably the worst thing they did overall though…were you a massage student? Did you ever wonder why the dumb kid that never tried in class somehow passed and graduated? Did you ever wonder why your instructors put up with their nonsense? Did you ever wonder why your class size dropped like flies then just suddenly plateaued? That's because if class sizes got too small, it literally became impossible to fail anyone. If the number of people in your class fell below a certain number, the entire group would be dropped. So, management would cook the books to avoid the hassle and continue making regular money. There are definitely licensed massage therapists out in the field that are frauds and know it. The system has failed.

Why I Hate Continuing Education Classes

Most states require licensing and they require additional training to maintain that licensing. Continuing education units (CEU's) ensure that practitioners are keeping their skill set above a certain standard. This is good for the client as any massage therapist they choose will have up to date training and skills. It doesn't really take much time, you could probably finish all the required hours in a couple of weekends, but I still absolutely dread it. Every. Single. Time.

There hasn't been a single CE class that I've been to where someone hasn't wanted to fight me or take me home. Its uncomfortable. Wildly uncomfortable. And to be clear, this is not the norm. Massage therapy classes are not known for being fight clubs or brothels—they're professional learning environments that are essential to a growing practice.

However, here's just a few of my bizarre interactions:

First class I went to after I graduated was a big seminar and I end up meeting a ton of other professionals. Good experience overall except for when I gave my number out to some guy and he about stalked me for the next week.

The time the teacher's assistant for a class was hitting on my wife and decided to wait for her afterwards. He even wanted to fight me to show off or something. Single guys out there, if you're considering this tactic, just stay home. I think he was shocked by the fact that nobody cared he was over six foot with hair. Didn't scare me and didn't impress my wife.

Or this one time when this guy trapped me in the restroom during a break from class and started asking me personal questions about me and my wife—the kind you'd ask someone to hack into their accounts. Like, there's no sly way of doing this either. *"So yeah, what street did you grow up on and, uh, what high school did your wife go to?"*

Or that one time when the teacher asked us to come up one by one and draw the organs on a blank body that was on white board. The guy before me purposefully drew the lungs to look like breasts and everyone had a good chuckle. Then I drew a liver, just your average liver, and the teacher made an example out of me because it was too small and "a real liver is WAY bigger than this." *Like okay, geesh, and lungs really look like breasts.* And it wasn't that much bigger. She just drew a line that outlined the image I drew. Like when you say its 4 o'clock and someone's like, *"Derrr, no its 3:58."*

Or the time I went to class to learn about relieving jaw pain. We were learning about an inner mouth protocol to help release the bound-up tissue around the jaw. You're supposed to glove up and dip your fingers in mouthwash solution to help further disinfect and lubricate the working surfaces. You should not just shove your ungloved index finger into someone's mouth and swirl your it around their tongue. My eyes about popped out of my head when that happened. Right in front of my wife and everything.

So yeah, I don't really look forward to these very much. But I'm sure I'm energetically responsible in some way for this—it all comes down to attitude. Control what you can, and don't sweat the rest.

My Favorite Part of the Job

Pain is the body's warning light. In short bursts, it is a necessary survival mechanism. *Ouch! Hot!* But when that warning light is constantly going off and is telling you about an injury you're already aware of but don't feel like you can do anything about—that's when it becomes maddening. That's when it becomes less of a tool for you and more of weapon against you. There's only so much time any one of us can withstand under constant pain before we're changed. I remember my father not smiling for years because of his chronic pain. And for so many it just gets worse with no end in sight. A vicious cycle.

My favorite part of what I do is being that little nudge in the right direction. That little force that leads to a domino effect of healing. The body wants to heal, it's actually very good at it, but sometimes it just needs some encouragement. I love seeing that spark of hope after someone's gotten off the table and can move without pain again. I love seeing them realize that it's not over, not yet it ain't. The fat lady has not sung!

It's easy to feel alone. It's easy to feel unheard. I want to listen, and I want to be there. I know how vulnerable one can feel when lying on the floor in crippling pain. Back in 2012, I was swimming in the ocean and was dragged to the bottom. A strong current had thrown me like a rag doll to the ocean floor and I landed on my head. I felt the rest of body whip around me in a flurry on impact. I remember feeling the back of my head touch my right shoulder blade. Immediately after, I felt the pull of the undertow start dragging me out to sea. My vision blurred and darkened. Almost instinctually, I felt the need to push off the dirt beneath me to burst to the surface. Any kid that's spent a lot of years in a pool knows the feeling. If I had passed out before the push or not felt that urge to push from the bottom, I'd be dead right now and you wouldn't be reading this awful book

94

(seriously though, thank you for reading). Ever since then, my back and neck require more attention and maintenance, or I end up as the guy on the floor in crippling pain. I want to be there for you before you get there. No one deserves to be in pain.

My second favorite part of the job is meeting all the animals. They have this understanding of the world that I cherish. I. Love. Animals. And ever since my horse reiki session, animals have connected with me a lot more. Yeah, no joke, totally had a reiki session with horses present. I normally have my reservations about energy workers, especially if they have a gimmick. But this was one of the most touching experiences of my life. I've taught many acupressure, chi gong, and meditation classes and I always hear about people seeing colors and images—I had never experienced this. I've felt more at peace with energetic modalities and meditation, but never saw anything. Then I had my horse reiki session.

For those of you who don't know, reiki sessions normally have little to no hands-on techniques present. It's a lot of the client laying on their back while the practitioner holds points, hovers above, or even draws symbols (there's even a whole section of transatlantic practices that focus on energy healing from very far away). But my horse reiki session took it to a whole new level. Not only did the horse lay its head on mine—we were nose to nose, nostril to nostril, but the horse also laid his head on every part of my body that was in pain. And I did see colors, I did see images. I saw all the colors of the rainbow blend into one another as a half-man/half-snake turned into a spider then that spider turned into millions of fractals of itself, and eventually there was nothing—it was trippy, and I highly recommend it.

Ever since then, animals have been so much more comfortable around me and me them. I don't know what that session did, but I'm cool wit' it.

How I Regenerate My Interest in Bodywork

It's common and natural for burn out to occur, even when you have everything in the right place. Humans need challenge and growth. Change is the only constant in life. You can't just put yourself on repeat and hope it will continue to be enough, eventually, it will catch up with you. Whenever I start feeling burnt out, there are three things I do to combat it:

1) I learn a new skill or revise a skill related to my field. Even after a decade in the industry, there's still plenty for me to learn, plenty for me to appreciate. Often there's a misconception of the black belt from a non-martial artists—it really doesn't mean master. It means a ready student. Yep, all those different colored belts you earn on your way to black are just different levels of novice. A black belt in this sense is just like white belt, but you're a 'true' student now. If you met a truly gangster black belt, their belt will have faded back to white. We should always be in a cycle revising and learning new skills. It doesn't mean I'm forgetting my foundation, but rather adding to it.

2) I become more charitable. Really anytime I become sad or burnt out, becoming more charitable can be a surefire way to get me excited again. In the past few years, my wife and I have started sponsoring and collecting books for Little Free Libraries throughout neighborhoods, collecting food for our local food bank, and many of our proceeds from book sales go towards The Humane Society (if you're an animal lover, be sure to check out my wife's book series 'That Fluffy Bitch', I guarantee it'll make you smile). Not just that, but at least for one month out of the year we give away free half hour sessions to preexisting clients and since meeting Jennifer Roseman, acupuncturist extraordinaire, all our upgrades are free. Cupping, guasha, kinesio-tape, CBD cream, aroma therapy, etc.—all free. And it feels gooooood.

3) I branch out and meet new friends or meet up with the ones I haven't connected with in a while. I guarantee you, there are professionals out there that you need to meet and be around. I call them giants and it's humbling to be in their presence. Even if I don't score some awesome connection or gain business, being around this type of person evokes this strong sense of will and might in me. They have a great drive about them while being able to see the whole (or most) of the battlefield. They have a healthy balance of not fearing the unknown while not blindly plunging themselves into anything unnecessary. The coolest part about this is when you become a giant for someone else and put them on your shoulder to see what you see.

Extra tip! Change your socks more. I change my socks at any chance I get to keep my mood stellar while working. Try it, you'll like the way you feel. I can't take full credit for this tip though, thank you, John!

Worst Thing I've Ever Done in a Massage Session! (Confession time! Yikes!)

Well…this is a disappointing chapter. Just skip it. I've been a pretty professional dude my whole career. The worst thing I've ever done in a massage is accidently physically assault somebody… in the face! Okay—here's the real story and it's not that juicy: I stood up from working on his neck, moved to one side of the body to work on something else, and for some damn reason just let my arms dangle as I moved and grazed his face with my hand. "Physically assaulted" seems to be far too radical of a term. We laughed about it. He even left me a raving review. BUT! I do know some awful stories that I've seen or been told.

1) Knew a lady who would take ecstasy before performing massage, said she gave a better session.

2) Know waaaaaaay too many massage therapists who want to talk about their day to me during my session. Like listen, I'm totally here for you…just not when I'm laying naked, face down on a table in pain. If you're reading this right now and you complain to your client while giving massage, I have this to say to you: It's perfectly understandable to be talkative with our clients, they are amazing people and some even want to hear about us and our lives, but please don't let out too much. Particularly if its negative. From a professional standpoint, I'd recommend keeping your points concise and keep more to asking about them or simply enjoy the silence. The session is about them. Please note, all experiences are different and there is no one size fits all, this is just my two cents.

3) Knew a gal that would take time off your massage. Like you pay for an hour and get 40 minutes. I don't know how she always pulled this off, but no one ever said a word.

4) Knew a girl who would text during her session. She would be massaging your feet with two hands, then you would kind of feel just one hand resting while the other disappeared. Not only is that totally disrespectful, but how damn gross. No. Just no.

5) Worked with a guy that would get so drunk during his shift, he would forget what room he put his client in. So, he would just go door to door hoping to find a room without a massage therapist in it. He lasted a surprisingly long time. It took several instances of this and then sleeping through a few clients' sessions before they let him go.

6) A lady was working on me once, used too much lotion, so wiped it off with a towel THEN USED THAT TOWEL TO WIPE THE SWEAT OFF HER FACE. GAAAH!

7) Heard about a lady that wouldn't massage tattooed areas because of the toxins. Like, if you came in for a fully body massage but had tattoos on your right arm, she'd massage everything but your right arm. What a damn loon.

Uh…yep…

What if I had Ultimate Power in the Massage Field?

If I had ultimate god-like powers and could control any facet of the massage industry, I'd ask for the acceptance of better music, less creeps, and fix how massage is marketed.

"Better music" is a bit of a joke—sometimes clients just have different tastes in music. But I'd love to hear more of the field listen to Little People, Gramatik, and DJ Shadow type artists or even just some Bossa Nova. I get that traditional massage music is married to the practice; it just seems like nobody actually likes it. Moreover, the evolution of traditional massage music is weird—whale noises, race car noises, it just ends up in a strange place. I've tried in the past to branch out while working at clinics (Thievery Corporation, not whale noises) but was sadly shot down very quickly. At the very least I'd like clients to be more forward about what they want to listen to. It doesn't always have to be bird noises and wind chimes over a babbling brook with some high-pitched synthesizer squeals.

"Less creeps" is a pretty standard wish...I think just about everyone would benefit from less creeps.

But how about marketing? What about that could change and why does it matter? Well, this dichotomy in the field of either you are spa oriented and focus on relaxation or you're in the pain management field and focus on results—they don't have to be two different paths. I think just saying you do one track or the other is likened to "I do half a job". In my very humble opinion, and I am **incredibly** humble, relax or results, luxury or medical type mindsets are fantastic places to start, but you should elevate yourself. Grow to a level of understanding to see the whole field and stop limiting yourself as a massage therapist.

And yes, yes, yes, I get it—some of us like focusing on just one part, that's fine. You shouldn't have to do something you don't want to and expressing yourself through one main avenue works well for some. You should be able to specialize in what you want. But recently I did a radio interview and one of the first questions they asked me was if I did "relaxation or therapeutic massage"—this is how the public sees us. This is what our marketing has limited us to. Either it feels good and doesn't really accomplish anything, or it hurts and gets the job done. The question reminded me of the physical therapist that told me they only focus on mobility and not pain management. How do you have one without the other? Now, I must admit that some parts of the massage field do require specialization, such as oncology massage, but it just seems like we're dividing up our own field to specialize in one part but it's the client/patients that suffer because of it.

All I'm saying is, why do we let our marketing limit us in our technique and why does there have to be such a strict split and lack of blend?

But trust me, our current marketing could improve regardless of my opinion. It's either pictures of overly green bamboo with balanced river rocks next to a purple flower **or** it's some blue x-ray of a guy holding his neck and has yellow and orange bursting from his spine and targets on his joints. And why does every massage therapist do that pose where they're looking over their shoulder at the camera with their arms crossed—and always with a blazer. **Always**. Is this really the best our industry can do? Is this how we really want ourselves represented? *Says the guy with a creep-ass cover.*

The Way of the King, and the King of the Way

This is the way of the 'Intercepting Raf', the way of the massage therapist.

Lift your back heel when moving forward; with hips as the vanguard. Your heel should be behind you during this movement, if it is under you, you will not lift the heel but instead kick the front leg forward to drag you along. This is a waste of power.

When stationary, if feet are together, you'll have the power of a feather.

When moving, heel to toe, or you'll lack flow.

To lower, bend knees or widen stance. Do not bend at your back.

Do not let your hips sag forward or back.

Both feet should point in the direction of applied force. When feet are in different directions, you will not lift your back heel. Until you master this, you will waste copious amounts of power.

Your hands needn't drastically differ in distance from your waist when applying force. If energy is generated from the heel and hips, then the hands only need to hold the weight. But when energy comes from the upper body only, there will be a change in distance from hips.

The further your hands travel from you, the weaker they become. The further your elbow travels from you, the weaker it becomes. Stack your tools, keep them close or under you. This is how the little river crashes like an ocean.

The tool holds its shape while movement is generated, the tool does not generate the movement. The shape is pliable yet sturdy.

We focus our technique towards the heart. From distal to proximal. From far to close. From fingertips to heart.

A stroke for the medial, a stroke for the middle, a stoke for the lateral. This is the intro to all segments.

You should be able to use every tool from your elbow down, and only that tool, throughout a full body massage. (e.g. using only elbows throughout a full body). These tools include the elbow and forearm, the ulnar side of the hand, the palm, the fist (soft), the knuckles (leopard's fist), and the fingertips. The brave will also learn how to use knees and heels. Do not become overly comfortable with one tool.

Your thumbs should stay close to your hand, especially when applying pressure. Shake out your hands and drop them to your side, this is the maximum distance your thumb should ever be from your palm when applying great force.

You should be able to apply to weight of a nickel and the weight of Mother Earth. On either spectrum, you should never be tense. Never hold a solid fist during massage.

Point your elbows down during forward moving techniques.

Gain mastery over your grip. From the base of the fingers to the thumb. From the tips of the fingers to the palm. From the tips of the fingers to the thumb. The gator, the monkey, and the snapping turtle.

Keep your head up and eyes on the horizon. There's no other position your head and eyes need to be in. Your head will remain up and your shoulders down.

You do not need your eyes for massage. You should be able to do a full body massage blindfolded. Over time, blindfolded and down to the very minute for an hour, hour and a half, and two-hour massage session. Time distorts during massage, the trained mind will not. Naturally, you must be able to set up and dress your table in this fashion too.

Let your mind wander, not aimlessly, but let it float and drift with the moment. Do not overthink your movements and intent; let them flow. If you have committed yourself to proper training, then you needn't worry. It's in this state that even the need to sneeze will not distract you. It's in this state that your touch will flow and crash like the ocean.

Do not revel in your work, flow to whatever is next without hesitation. It is in this fashion that you will discover the infinite strokes and eight palm illusion.

Be bountiful in your technique, do not waste time with that which does not serve you.

Heavy is followed by light, press followed by pull, lateral followed by medial.

Liken your touch to water. Enter space without making a ripple. Flow with ease and without prejudice. From a trickle, to the weight of the ocean. To and back again, like the tide.

Do not drape your client from the head of the table.

Thank your client after each session for allowing you to perform your craft on them.

When at home, you must continue to exercise your hands. You must train yourself to endure.

Do not short yourself on sleep. Do not short yourself on calories.

This is the way of the King and the King of the way.

IV

Ouroboros
and the Titan's Hunger

FAQ

Do your hands ever hurt?

> They did. For the first seven years. I did a lot of
> conditioning to improve grip strength and overall hand
> health. Also, this might sound odd, but I drank a lot of
> eggshell and gelatin powder. Heard from an NFL player
> and doctor that that would help my joints. So, I drank
> that gross mixture every day for years and I still don't
> know if it was that or the training, but I don't hurt
> anymore.

Do you massage fat people?

> I work with all body types and with an ample amount of
> respect. But no, the massage doesn't really differ all that
> much from a petite person to a large person. That's often
> times what people are asking when this question comes
> up. "Are there differences in technique you use for
> different body types?" or "what are the limitations of
> your technique when working with certain body types?"
> are probably better worded versions of this question.

What's the weirdest thing that's ever happened during a
massage?

> A dog trying to aggressively hump me while making eye
> contact. I don't recommend it.

What's the scariest thing that's ever happened while making a
house call?

> The client's house I was at had a motion light that would
> lock onto and follow any movement. It was dark and
> raining when I was leaving and the light was following
> me, but every couple of seconds it would dart over and
> lock onto a dark patch (even the light pointed directly at

it didn't make a difference), move slightly, then stop and lock back onto my movement. Almost like someone or something was moving towards me, then would pause when noticed. My imagination went wild with possibilities and I hurried to my car. I locked the doors and turned my car to face the dark patch that the motion light kept locking onto—to find nothing. No one at all. Sometimes the scariest things are all in our head.

Masseuse or massage therapist?

Industry professionals normally appreciate 'massage therapist'. The term 'masseuse' has been attached to prostitutes that have used massage therapy as a front for their activities. Using 'massage therapist' helps create a distinction between professional and not so professional services. But I find because of this, massage therapists take way too much offense to the term. It's still a generally used term to describe the professionals in our field and some of the public hasn't caught on yet. We're living in a politically correct society, but it can still take time for people to catch on. My only real problem with the phrase is it literally translates to "a woman that performs massage therapy." I am a man. 'A masseur'.

Ice or heat?

Do you put ice or heat on an injury? This is a really common question and even in this modern age of medicine, science and the internet, it still seems up for debate. Normally when asked this question, my answer is: **movement**. Although it seems counterintuitive, your body uses movement to heal. You must have it. This isn't the first time in this booked I've mentioned how important movement is. And it shouldn't be substituted. But what if you have a hard time moving due to your injury? Then what? I still feel there's better measures out there for injury recovery than thermotherapy, but it does have its place and we'll talk about that soon. But in short, on either side of the debate you have those who swear by what they use, but my recommendation is either heat treatments or short ice treatments (like under a minute) or preferably alternating between the two. I don't recommend long ice treatments for soft tissue recovery, but everyone has something that works for them. But here's why my recommendation is the way that it is. You can't expect to heal without blood flow, long heat and short ice treatments can encourage this. Your body's initial reaction to something cold is to combat it with more warmth (circulation), but this response fades and even begins to shut down nervous signals, which is fine for pain management, but may delay the actual healing process. And although long heat treatments have been said to pool blood in an injured area, its focus is more to relax the blood vessels and allow for the more than usual number of cells (mostly white blood cells - WBC's) to enter the injured site. But, if heat is drawing blood there, what's then syphoning it back away from the injured site? This is another good reason to contrast your thermal therapy treatments, it makes it complete. Because remember, it's all about circulation. You gotta have dat circulation.

But what else would Raf recommend for recovering from an injury if ice and heat aren't as great as we thought them to be? Do you remember when you were a kid on the football team or maybe it was in a 1st Aid class, but you may have learned about the RICE method? It stands for rest, ice, compression, and elevation. I'm sure many of you used it at one point to attempt a hastier recovery. Dr. Gabe Mirkin coined the term in the 1970's and almost immediately after began trying to convince people it didn't work, because it doesn't. Yeah, he thought he was onto the mac daddy of soft tissue recovery protocols until he found out that half of the recipe can actually make for a slower healing process, instead. Rest and ice, the first two in the acronym, are the two culprits here in question. Sure, actual sleep is needed for recovery, but when you're awake **YOU NEED TO MOVE**. Even if it's a small amount, the body needs some direction in the healing process and movement is the director. Without moving an injured site, scar tissue lays randomly for optimal support, this is not necessarily conducive to movement later on though. If you move while healing, your scar tissue has a better chance of forming along fibers, meaning you'll have support with a lower possibility of losing range of motion. Might I also mention, swelling will have a much harder time decreasing without movement and compression. (I don't knock the second half of RICE, but we've got to forget the first half.)

So…if not RICE, then what? MEAT. And despite its name, it's actually vegan friendly (okay that was a bad joke, it's alright if you just stop reading here). It stands for movement, exercise, analgesic, and treatment. Yeah, movement, that thing that my whole career revolves around. But what's the difference between movement and exercise? Think small to big, partial to full—you graduate to exercises after movement. Just because you can move something again, doesn't mean it's up to full strength, which means it's still susceptible to injury. You might just have to restart the whole healing process over because you didn't take your exercises seriously.

Analgesic refers to a drug to helps relieve pain. This doesn't have to come in pill form or be a major pain killer, something like a topical analgesic is perfect—biofreeze, tiger balm, something you rub across the skin over the affected area. Anything like this is super useful during your recovery. By reducing the amount of pain you experience, you'll have a much better chance of accomplishing the first half of the MEAT acronym. Most of the time, this is why heat or ice are being used anyways— to alleviate pain. The big differences being you don't have to walk around with a bag of heat or ice.

Now, onto to treatment. You'll have a much more rapid healing time if you get treated by a professional. There are so many wonderful practices out there that can help: acupuncture, chiropractic, massage therapy, gua sha, cupping, even using a big resistance band to floss out the affected area –this has also been referred to as 'muscle flossing' or 'voodoo flossing' because it works like magic. If you're unfamiliar, it's a simple process of wrapping a long resistance band around a joint or segment, starting away from heart and wrapping towards the heart. For example, you'd wrap ankle to knee/ wrist to elbow. After you've wrapped the area, do all the motions, especially the ones that are hard for you. The band helps to create friction and compression as you take yourself through movement. This is great for increasing blood flow and breaking up adhered tissue. Just search it on YouTube, you'll get pages of videos.

But Raf, haven't you heard of the cryochambers that the NBA players use? I have and I'm all jelly (that's a millennial term for 'jealous' if you're wondering). I'd love to try it out! But what's the difference? IS there *actually* a difference? Why does one work and the other doesn't? Well, if they could just use bags of ice and get the same effect, then I'm sure they would (it's an ungodly amount of money for a treatment). But this is far more effective in a much shorter time span. BUT WHY? Because the cryochamber drops to minus 250 degrees Fahrenheit while your bag of ice is like 32. The chamber is doing what a bag of ice claims to do: push inflammation out of an injured site. It's a bag of ice on steroids that ate a bag of ice on steroids.

Side note - Before we wrap this "ice or heat" discussion, I'd like to quickly mention a little benefit of ice that you may want to look into: weight loss. Tim Ferris in his book 'The Four Hour Body' mentions how a man lost double the weight in half the time by taking ice baths and drinking cold water. Supposedly the temperature difference forced his body to burn more calories (another example he gives is Michael Phelps eating 12,000 calories a day because his time in a cold pool increases the amount he burns requiring more fuel). Now, **I'm not here to give you dieting advice or teach you about weight loss,** there's other professionals out there far more qualified for that, but since we were on the subject, I just wanted to point you in the direction of a resource. I know how much easier it is to move once you've lost a few extra pounds. I went from 225 to 170 in just a few months. It was a big transformation and I credit some of that to cold showers and ice baths. My knees stopped hurting and I could touch my toes again without making old man noises. It really is the simple things that can help us move pain free.

Do you massage sweaty people?

Yes. We're at sporting events all the time.

Do you massage feet?

Yes, of course. Like one of my old instructors used to say, "no massage is complete, without the hands and feet." But it is a valid question because I personally know massage therapists (even ones with more experience than me) that don't touch the feet. They think its *gross*. Like they have cooties or something.

Do you have time for an extra hour?

Sometimes I do and it can't hurt to ask. We try to always allow time for last minute changes, we get how life can be. That's the beauty of being my own boss, I can make those calls and don't have to run it by someone else.

Do you like office or mobile massage better?

> We had an office attached to our home; it was awesome. Made for a short drive to work and meant we could pack much more into our day without the drive time. But it also meant that guests might show up without having an appointment scheduled.

> I'm a much bigger fan of the mobile gig. I love seeing peoples' homes and meeting their family and animals. I love traveling across this beautiful part of Arizona (Prescott quad-city area). But I especially love how the client doesn't have to sit in a car afterwards. We just spent an hour or so stretching the body out, only to have it shorten up on the car ride home—not preferable.

How often should I get massage?

> Of course, everyone is different. But here's my simple guide to how often you should schedule a massage appointment:

> > In lots of pain and have a hard time moving –

> > 2-3 times per week

> > In lots of pain but can manage movement –

> > once per week

> > Minor to moderate pain is present (especially for those with active schedules) –

> > one every two weeks

> > Minor aches to pain free –

> > once per month

> I personally like to get treatments once every two weeks, even if I'm feeling good. Your body is an adapting machine and will do anything to keep you going, even if

that means compromising posture and joint health that will have an impact later. These changes can be insidious and when you start to notice them, it's already a lot of work to correct them. Getting massage frequently not only helps the body heal but brings awareness as well. Most people have no idea what's going on in their own body, it's no wonder why many of us end up with poor posture and achy joints. The earlier you recognize this, the better. Regular massage can help with this.

Do you get hit on a lot?

Not *a lot*, but much more than my wife does. Ow oww! Even once had a guy ask me if I did "intense anal massage". Now, one thing you have to understand about me, is I am the definition of socially awkward and rarely do I understand when someone is hitting on me or making fun of me. So, knowing my downfall, I try and always give people the benefit of the doubt. Maybe he meant his gluteal muscles? He didn't mean his glutes. He clarified.

How do I feel about surgeries and pain meds?

You do what you gotta do. Most people think I oppose surgeries and pain medication, but it's quite the opposite actually. Of course, my job is to help you move pain free without pharmaceuticals and surgeries, but if you need those things to get through your day, then do it. Surgeries are meant to correct an issue and pain meds are available for those of us who can't take time to stop our life for an injury. We have to focus on the now before we can worry about the later.

Besides, just because you got a surgery or are taking pain meds doesn't mean we can't hang out, in fact, again, quite the opposite. Post-surgery massage is a real thing and it can definitely help with the recovery process. Even though your very talented doctor has corrected an issue, the body needs time to heal and adjust, and massage therapy can help with that. Massage therapists are here to support you in any part of your wellness journey.

Do men ever get…*erections* while getting a massage?

Yes, but not in the way you're thinking. So, when your client has an erection, there's one thing you need to determine before continuing the massage and it takes no time at all: what's their intent? If they're sawing logs and passed out, then don't worry about it and move on. This is natural and happens often. Massage therapy can help you hit your REM cycle much faster than usual, and it's in this portion of sleep that blood pressure changes and you can unconsciously end up with an erection. Happens like 5 - 6 times a night for most men. Like seriously, it's no big deal. (BTW! I totally had a woman wake me up in a massage and mention to me I had an erection. She then said, "I'll give you a minute to take care of that." And then just left the room. Understand, I was sound asleep just before this. *You woke me up because I have a what? And you want me to 'take care of it'? What does that mean? And why would it only take me a minute?* So many questions. Not a very relaxing and therapeutic experience.) But if they're staring at you, rubbing their nipples, with an erection, then yes you end the session and leave. This unfortunately happened to a colleague of mine.

Do you ever see people naked?

No, gross. We make every effort possible to ensure our clients privacy and decency are respected. People are already in a vulnerable position when getting bodywork, they don't need to also worry if some pervert is working on them or not.

Do you have to go to school?

> In most states, yes. But the amount of training hours differs from state to state. Some states don't require any licensing at all. You can just wake up one day and BE a massage therapist.

Why do massage therapists have to have a license?

> Not every state requires a license to practice massage, and in fact, there are easy work arounds in some states that do require a license. I don't recommend either of these routes. Go to school, take your training seriously. The license we carry is to benefit those around us—in multiple ways. With training, we create a standard, and with a standard we create trust. But possibly the most important reason to have a license and to abide by the law, is because of its usefulness in combating human trafficking. It's not something you normally think about when talking about licenses. But this is a tool law enforcement can use to shut down 'massage parlors' (those are the gross ones that double as brothels) and ensure the safety of those forced into it. When I first got licensed, I had some rather libertarian views on the matter, but this world is so much bigger (and scarier) than me. And I'll gladly pay, qualify for, and maintain a license if it means someone gets to avoid a terrible life.

> Also, it keeps your edge sharp. Slacking on training is common for everyone as soon as you graduate, just remember that it can catch up with you. Doing the required training helps you to avoid that slump.

What is a knot? Like, what *is* it?

> In short, it's part of a muscle throwing a temper tantrum. But according to the goddess of trigger point (TrP) therapy, Janet G. Travell, MD (yeah, the same Janet G. Travell, MD that was the physician for President John F.

Kennedy), a TrP is defined as "a hyperirritable spot in skeletal muscle that is associated with a hypersensitive palpable nodule in a taut band. The spot is tender when pressed and can give rise to characteristic referred pain, motor dysfunction, and autonomic phenomena."
Basically, it's a micro-cramp that can send a predictable pathway of pain through the body and can be caused by impact, overuse, dehydration or lack of proper nutrients.

Why did I cut my hair?

I shave my head, I used to have long hair; a braided ponytail that went down to my waist. When my wife and I started our business, we started doing videos with a body builder who was sponsored by a production company that had a rather large following. After watching the first video we did together, all I could think was, "Daaaaaamn, I'm ugly as all hell. Does my hair really look like *that*?" I looked like an even creepier version of the butler from Scary Movie 2—*"I better use my strong hand."* So, after watching that video, I walked into my bathroom and cut it all off. Went for the Lex Luthor look instead, and I've been beautiful ever since.

What are your pet peeves in massage?

There's really not much about the client that bothers me. If there ever is a time I am bothered, then I reflect inwardly and figure out the cause (most of the time it's because I'm 'hangry'). Any annoyance I do come across normally manifests itself in the form of robocallers or terrible drivers. The client deserves to have the utmost support and understanding. We don't have room for annoyance. Now yes, there are clients I've come across that were the definition of rude. And yes, I have had to draw the line before. But I often feel when people talk about pet peeves it's in relation to an everyday occurrence. Like you're training yourself to overreact to a quality or situation, when instead you should be reacting case by case. The cookie cutter mentality is inflexible and brittle. Like a Bruce Lee once said, "flow like water, my friend."

Have your tattoos ever stopped you from getting work?

I have a full sleeve and my neck tattooed, also my chest, ribs, thigh, and back of my shoulder but you can't see those. In my experience, the only people that make a fuss over tattoos are managers and people that don't have tattoos, but watch shows about them (LA Ink and shows like that). I actually find that clients are more offended by managers forcing people to cover up tattoos rather than just letting it be.

The worst thing anyone has ever said to me, in context to professionalism and tattoos, was from the president of an insurance company who said, "If it came down to hiring you or someone equally as qualified who didn't have tattoos, I'd have to go with them." Implying that either one of us would get the job if we were more qualified than the other. Which sounds fair to me.

Is there a way to tell if your massage therapist will be good or not?

This is highly subjective of course, but I feel vetting out the competency of your practitioner comes down to two things:

1) Does anyone talk about them? Word of mouth is powerful and if you're good enough, people will tell their friends and post about their experience online. Now, understand that this isn't always a reliable credential—what if they're new to the field? And living in an age of modern technology, what can you really

believe online? There're bots for everything nowadays and it seems there's still a lack of accountability in the online world.

2) The more important credential, however, is the conversation before getting on the table. Are they listening to you? Like, actually listening. Not just hearing but listening and confirming. You should feel like you are the only concern for your practitioner in the whole world (which is rather therapeutic for the massage therapist as well. In a time when it seems like the world is always on the brink of destruction and Nazis are still somehow a thing, it's nice to be able to just focus on one set of issues.). No joke, I went to a clinic once to get a massage and told my massage therapist I needed focus on my hips and quads—I knew for a fact that that was creating my issues. She responded with, "we're going to go through the whole body, so if we have time, we'll spend a few extra minutes on those areas." I knew this was going to be a crap massage. This mentality normally comes from a new practitioner, fresh out of school. While in training, it's common to emphasize working the entire chain of connective tissue and muscle to fully alleviate the problem. The issue with that is it can lead to an overzealous mindset that overlooks the client's wants/needs.

Now of course, your massage therapist should recommend treatment plans and what they think the best course of action is, but to tell you out loud that they will be ignoring what you feel in pursuit of their own goals, is a major red flag.

P.S. The Arizona Massage Board has a portion of their site dedicated to formal complaints against massage therapists. Although it is a resource for the clients, understand I've hired people with formal complaints filed against them. It can range from the very serious to the incredibly minor. I knew a guy that had a miscommunication with his client that lead to a formal complaint. Knew another guy who didn't turn his documentation in for continuing education hours and is now on the wall of shame. I'm not saying the AZ Massage Board is a sham, I'm just saying to use your reason with this resource.

What advice would you give to a massage therapist just starting out?

Be open to feedback, but trust in your training. You have so much room to grow, but remember, you are the professional here. You are responsible for interpretation of the feedback given to you from the body on the table. You must turn it into something useful. Brief example, I was trained to work in the lamina groove. This is the groove created along your spine that's in between the spinous and transverse processes (just to either side of the bumps you can feel on your back). There are a lot of muscles that attach in this area and you can relieve a lot of tension with massage. I was working in this area on another massage therapist and she grunted, "*You're. On. My. Spine.*", I did the same move on a doctor and he said, "oh wow, I didn't think massage therapists knew how to work in there. That's amazing!" So have faith in your technique and understand feedback in a way that can benefit you. It wasn't that I was on a bone, even though she mentioned a bone (90% of massage therapy relies on pressing tissue into bone) but she was either trying to tell me to have more finesse as I worked or that that area was extremely tender and to back off. Either way, it didn't mean I should stop doing the technique altogether, but that I needed to tailor it better to each spine. It just needed to be refined. Basically, don't allow fear and frustration to guide your interpreting mind, come from a place of reason. *Wow, he says that a lot.*

Did you meet your wife in massage school?

I did. I was an instructor, and she a student—oh yes, boys and girls, this is a story of forbidden love and sacrifice. I had never seen a more beautiful being in my entire life, and I have been to many places. She's the kind of beautiful that male authors portray when writing about female characters. The first day of class, I pulled my TA aside and told him I knew I was going marry Linda King someday, I just knew it. But I also loved my job (I know it may not have sounded liked it when you read previous chapters, but I did). And there was no way I was going to jeopardize my position, credibility, or her education. So, from then until the day she graduated, I did my best to ignore her. Can you imagine trying to ignore the one person who makes your heart race all the while feeling like you've known them for eons? It was maddening to a degree. I did everything in my power to avoid her, but she was smart. She respected that we couldn't be together while she was a student and I an instructor, but she always had some lame question to ask me that I knew she had the answer to already. Inevitably, it would still lead into a whole conversation—I think she liked seeing the embarrassed look on my face when I realized I had been speaking with her for too long and too candidly. What can I say? She brings the goofy side out of me.

But, because I was essentially off the table, she did what anyone would do; she moved on. She started dating some former special forces army guy. And I mean this guy had the looks, the muscles, the tattoos, the nice car, loads of money—then there's me. *wipes crumbs off of shirt* Like, there seriously wasn't any comparing the two of us. (insert your favorite "you vs. the guy she tells you not to worry about" meme here) Have you ever bought a frozen pizza because the picture on the box looked really good but then you get home and throw it in

120

the oven only to realize it's just a sad, sad parody of what was advertised?—yeah, that's me and this other guy. I'm the sad parody here.

I was a bit heartbroken, but I knew it was for the best. I was dedicated to my job and had a duty to uphold. I couldn't form a relationship with her and that was that. The world keeps on spinning. I can't say I really took it like a champ though. There are just some things in this life that cut deep. And understanding that I'd never be with her hurt like no other. But I knew what I signed up for. And I know the only way to truly put something behind you, is to push through it. So that's what I did. I showed up to work every day and kept doing what I do like a damn professional.

But then, days before graduation a staff member came up to me and said, "You know…you and Linda would make a cute couple."

My stomach sank; I felt like they were mocking me. The staff was notorious for spreading rumors based on very little (it got so bad that a husband and wife worked on the team, and one day the husband yelled at her, "IS THAT HOW YOU TALK ABOUT ME WHEN I'M NOT IN THE ROOM?!" Then stormed off.) and I thought someone had pieced something together. I tried so hard to avoid any mess and I thought it was about to hit the fan. I thought I failed an angel that forgot about me.

Then the sweetest words, "because I told her that and she thinks so too." She hadn't forgotten. She hadn't moved on.

The night of her graduation she was far more direct than before. She asked me out on a date, I said yes, and two weeks later we moved in together. Life's been perfect ever since.

The moral of the story is: life is exactly how it is in the movies and you should believe everything you see on T.V.

Why do you except food from clients?

Because it's normally really good food and I love and trust my clients. I understand that some individuals may have food allergies and can't just eat whatever is handed to them (even my brother has celiac disease), but I eat like I'm refueling the DeLorean from Back to the Future, like a human dumpster. I bring this up because I've been confronted so many times about it by other massage therapists. Even had a roommate once look at me in disgust as I came home with cookies from a client's home. "How can you eat that?! You don't even know what's in it! Or who made it!", he said while eating a bean burrito from Taco Bell (this was just before he tore into a bag of sour patch kids). I just always love the rationale that a big company that doesn't even know who you are would *never* screw you over and definitely cares about you, but someone I've come to consider a friend is going to put rusty nails or rat poison in the batch of cookies they gave me. (While we're at it, can someone explain why it's okay on Halloween to dress up as Satan and take candy from strangers but not any other day of the year?)

I often get asked if I'm afraid that my clients are going to drug me and kidnap me. Listen, yeah, use your wits and observe your surroundings because it is a crazy world out there and all that shit can definitely happen to you. But, like, no, I'm totally not scared of a client that's missed two days of work and can barely stand to answer the front door…I mean, yeaaah, *surely*, they have this sinister master plan to pretend to be injured, gain my trust, and then drug me so they can lock me in their basement (ya'll seen to many bad horror movies), because I'm just so cute and worth so much money.

I'm not scared of taking food from people I trust; I am however, scared of this next question.

How do you let your wife travel to strangers' homes?

First off, my wife will do what she pleases. She is a strong, powerful, independent woman and no man will contain her. But again, I think this is a simple case of rewording. "How do I handle my wife traveling to strangers' homes for work?" Of course, in the back of my mind, I naturally worry about the worst. There are evils that lurk in this world, but that doesn't mean we should hide, it means we should prepare. And that's exactly what we do. We've gone over some of the worst scenarios that could happen and train with self-defense instructors. I know my wife could whoop your wife, and then you. On top of that, we meticulously document addresses and even have a system that tracks our whereabouts and how long we've been there.

I've had friends ask me in the past if by preparing for something bad to happen, am I asking for the universe to send us trouble? I can see their point, but I don't feel this is a 'Master Oogway' situation, "one often meets his destiny on the road to avoid it"—in fact, quite the opposite BUT you must be mindful of it. Let me explain: We used to watch self-defense videos every day on our lunch. In these videos, they'd break down real life conflicts and what the victim did right and wrong during their response to an attacker. Although the purpose of these videos was to prepare us for the unknown and for life-threatening situations, there's only so many of these you can watch before you're irrationally angry at anyone you don't know. Everyone becomes a potential attacker and your perception of people changes. I feel this is a mentality that can be taken too far.

People stopped talking to me, this is what one of my self-defense instructors called 'creating a fuck off perimeter', which much as it sounds, is creating a boundary with your attitude to keep people away from you. If people are away, they can't hurt you. Again, I feel this is a bit extreme and can over sensationalize any conflicts that do occur. It's mentalities like this that create 'shooting someone in the back because of a misunderstanding' type situations.

So, what did we do? We stopped watching the videos as much and replaced them with something more wholesome, but we didn't forget the lessons that were intended to be passed along and this is really we're self-defense training shines. Yes, you need to train physically, and you need sparring time, but focusing on the cues, the red flags of a bad situation are so much more important. Noticing an attacker before you have to go toe to toe with them is SO much more preferable. An example: it's become common practice for criminals to bait you with money on your windshield, then bash you over the head and steal your stuff. Knowing what tactics may be employed might save you the headache of dealing with a serious situation.

I may not feel totally comfortable with my wife traveling to strangers' homes, but I know we've done everything in our power to prepare, and these are the best odds we get to work with.

Blurbs, Rants, and Raves

Marketing at gyms can be ideal. Clients there are focused on pain free movement, just like the massage therapist is. And I have a super simple method to marketing and you should copy it: I hang out and provide a service for free (I think it's a pretty amazing service, but I am super biased). And by hang out, I mean really—I leave a sign up that says, "free massage", I have a chair or a table out that is quite obviously used for massage, some business cards around, and I just chill and wait for someone to ask me about my craft. It works well. Turns out people who don't look at you also don't want to talk to you. And people who want something from you might just come up and ask. I know…it's craaaazy.

So, there I was, doin' my thang, and I notice an older woman walk into the gym. She walks directly up to my table and says not once, not twice, but boy oh boy, THRICE, "I would *neva!*" I know you read that quote and imagined a wagging finger to go along with it. It was there, I saw, inches from my face. She was disgusted at the thought of free massage being offered in a gym she went to. She also felt the need to tell me on the way out, as well. And of course, before the lobby doors shut behind her on her way out, she gave me one more, "I would *nevaaaaaa…*"

Like…okay? Then don't?

––––––––––––

When my girlfriend dumped me for joining massage school.

––––––––––––

When my girlfriend (different one) dumped me for working as a massage therapist—she was one too. She was a strange one.

———————

We were at an event giving free massage and a lady walked by our 'free massage' sign and whispered, "*how rude*". But that kind of whisper that old people do when they forget how to whisper and it's just a loud, raspy voice instead. Firstly, what do people think we do? And secondly, why wouldn't we be able to hear them?

———————

By invite, went to a boxing gym for their monthly customer appreciation day. We were going to be giving free massage to their members. It was held on the third Thursday of every month. It was easy enough to remember, "third Thursday", they even sound the same. When we showed up, the manager, at first, tried telling us it wasn't the third Thursday of the month. Once we pulled out a calendar and helped her count to three, she then changed her story to the customer appreciation day is on the fourth Thursday—because that rhymes and makes sense? I don't know why she just didn't tell us she forgot or didn't like us. We never went back, homie don't play dat.

———————

The time I set up next to my aunt at a marketing event, and it took her over an hour to recognize me…I even said, "Hi aunt blah blah blah" and she just looked at me. I don't think my family loves me. I just have one of those faces, ya know?

———————

Once saw a childhood friend at a marketing event. It was remarkable, we hadn't seen one another in over ten years. The only thing she said to me was she had a boyfriend, then left. Yep, one of those faces…

———————

The time I paid to do chair massage at an event (don't ever do this, btw), and they said I couldn't because *points to people feet away from me* "They're doing it." These people let us into the event and took our money with the knowledge that we are a mobile massage company and this what we do—they thought we just wanted to sit and talk about how awesome massage feels. *Not the brightest bulb in the pack, huh?*

Got to talking to the other massage therapists there (that could massage) and found out that with all their experience combined, it came out to half of mine. The definition of 'frustrating' is watching a bunch of noobs while you're forced to take a time out.

———————

I was at the store waiting in line to buy my groceries when the guy behind me inquired about my shirt (spa's name and logo were on it). Once he found out I was a massage therapist he said to me, "Must be nice layin' around all day getting paid to get massaged…" That's—that's not how it…oh never mind.

———————

Shout out to Darci Nakagawa for always going out of her way to help us with marketing. You never asked for a single cent in compensation. I miss you friend and hope you're enjoying the book. Tell the fam I said hi.

Was once at a big marketing event held in a parking lot. As we were getting set up, my wife dropped our tip jar and it shattered on the asphalt. No biggie, I asked her to grab a broom and get it cleaned up while I finished setting up. My wife is a very rebellious woman, so naturally, she just starts PICKING UP THE GLASS WITH HER FREAKING HANDS. She owns and operates the massage company with me, by picking up that glass WITH HER FREAKING HANDS she was risking well over half of our income.

So, I said to her in a panic, "WOMAN!" and she replied, "*Don't yell at me in public.*"

Now, do you remember from earlier in the book when I mentioned I don't pick up on social cues very well? Yeah, this is one of those times. The qualifier of "in public" made it sound like it was okay to yell at my wife at home, just not in public— like I'm some crazy wife beating maniac that is making progress by not yelling at her in public so we can celebrate by keeping the abuse to just our private life. Yeaaaah. **I treat my wife good, damn good**. But in this moment, on the assumption that I did not treat my wife good, everyone there wanted to kick my teeth in. I got glares and stares all day. I'm talking the marines, these huge personal trainers, oddly big face painters, even the chiropractors—and I was oblivious to all of it. Totally didn't understand why no one would talk to me after that.

Oh yeah, and to make matters worse my wife had an appointment in the middle of this event, so it looked like she got mad and left me there.

It wasn't till after we left that I put it all together, though. *Oh… that's why everyone was staring at me murderously…and shunned me…*

Now, to explain, I've talked this over with my wife and we both don't know why she chose those words to verbalize how she was feeling. The best we could come up with is that we had been watching too many sappy movies and should probably watch something with stronger female role models.

Hired a gal who quit after her first session. The hiring process took weeks and she quit after an hour.

So, I really try not to hate on multi-level marketing (MLM's) companies. In fact, when I first started my mobile business with my wife, we earnestly tried to help as many MLM individuals as possible. We would email out events we were going to and send people to chat with them as much as possible; I'm a firm believer in you get what you give. But it seemed like every time we tried getting more involved this would always happen: "well hey, let's meet for lunch and see how we can benefit each other." I'm so down for symbiotic relationships. BUT. EVERY. FREAKING. TIME. I'd show up for lunch ready to brainstorm some cool strategies and ideas, and they'd whip out the lab top and have me watch a 15-minute video on their product and how getting in their down chain can make me so much money. And then, without fail, every time, they would mention how much clients trust me and how easy it would be for me to sell to them. I genuinely want to help others out, but it becomes a chore when they start looking at you like you're some kind of sucker. Regardless, I wish the best to all MLMer's. It's tough out there and we all gotta eat.

Let me tell you about the worst massage I've ever had. I should've known. There are just somethings that you don't skimp on price with. Paying less isn't always a good thing (tattoos are a good example). But they advertised inexpensive treatments for the head, neck, and feet in 30-minute increments and it sounded exactly like what my wife and I needed. The place had good reviews and the owner even greeted us at the door. He even took the time to explain to us how the treatment would go, "they'll start on the head then work on the neck and finish with the feet. You can leave your belongings here and just sit back and relax." Any apprehensions I had before started to alleviate. Maybe this place was legit? Then the massage started.

I was expecting a massage of the head, neck, and feet. So, you can understand my shock when our "massage therapists" came in and barked at me to take off my shirt and lie face down. So obviously, being the rational, assertive man, I am— I just did it. I took my shirt off and lied face down. They began to work on my back (which if you've been keeping up so far, was not in the plan) but 'work' is too polite of a word. She assaulted me with pseudo massage techniques. When she had her fun there, she asked me to flip over and she put a blind fold on me. I could see out of the bottom on the blindfold though, and lying down, meant I could see the foot of the table and the entrance of the room. This is an important detail because at one point my "massage therapist" poked at one of my tattoos, laughed, then just left the fucking room only for a completely different woman to enter and finish the "treatment".

Why didn't you just stop the session if it was so awful? I honestly thought my wife's session had to be going better than me. I looked over a couple times and she looked like she was enjoying herself. How could I bring myself to ruin her session because mine was subpar? It's just a half hour. Well, *ding ding ding* I was wrong again. Her session was as terrible too.

So, we finish and pay for our voluntary assault, only to be exposed to the pièce de résistance, the icing on the cake, the crown jewel, the magnum opus—cigarette smoke to the face. Oh yeah, baby. The lady who was the first one to "work" on me, was smoking a cigarette by the door, like in the doorway and made sure to shotgun blast that into my lungs, "Come again! Have nice day!"

Places like this normally operate under one person's license. I don't know how they get away with it. The massage board in my state has suspended people for a lot less. But I'm sure there's some crafty loophole they're utilizing to make the massage board look like a bunch powerless chumps. Sometimes I don't understand bureaucracy or why I'm held to standards, but others aren't.

Moral of the story: speak up. Even licensed practitioners may perform techniques that don't jive with you, speak up. I often like to make the cheesy joke with my clients, "I haven't been married long enough to develop my mind-reading abilities yet, so you'll have to let me know when I need to change something." Its cheesy, but it works. Without proper communication, and even with good intent, you can end up feeling disappointed in a treatment. Many massage therapists use a degree of intuition during their work, but it always helps to have room for dialogue to be open.

Oh hey, how about an honorable mention? I was getting a massage from an older coworker and she decided to grab and pull both my nipples at the same time. And then she got mad that I got mad. Like I was disrespecting her for not letting her yank on my nipples. Double you tee ef?

———————————

Once worked with a gal who thought pregnancy massage was bad for you. I hate morons like this.

I will not drive with you if we're going to California. I've been on way too many business trips where I present my one condition and it goes unheard: we will not go to the beach on our last day here. Carve out an extra day prior to when our duties begin or go sometime during our trip, but just not the last day. FOR THE LOVE OF GOD, NOT ON THE LAST DAY. Because here's what happens, every single damn time. We go to the beach after business is wrapped up and hang out till the sun sets, then we drive home and don't get back until like 1 or 2 in the morning—and of course, everyone plans to work the next day and have to get up in a few hours. But the rationale is always to same, "*Oh c'mon, live a little! You can't just come to Cali and not see the beach!*" Lol ok.

That time we got invited to work at The Vans Warped Tour, only to find out they wanted to keep half of the tip money we made followed by half of what we made from future visits from clients that we met while there. Meaning, if I met you at Warped Tour, I was then expected to continually pay this company half of whatever you paid me, in perpetuity. In the censored words on my man, Ceelo Green, "forget you and forget you too."

I drive a lot for my work. I spend a decent amount of time on the road. For every hour of massage, there's close to an hour of driving. I'll just get to the point on this one, ya'll need to drive better. Your blinker is not a mid-lane change tool used to indicate what I already know, because half your vehicle is already in my lane. Moreover, I can't read your mind when you

132

want to lane change. If only there was some piece of sophisticated technology that signaled to me when you wanted to change lanes?

Also, quit rubber necking. Traffic was backed up for miles the other day all because AN ENTIRE CITY of lookie-loos had to get their fix—the accident wasn't even blocking any lanes. I'm going to tell you what Hank Williams and Delta 5 have been telling people for years now: mind your own business.

AND ANOTHER THING! The left lane is for passing and the right is for literally anything else. But God forbid if someone tries passing you. And while I'm at it, stay off your phones. It's irritating that cars have been around for so long and yet, rarely do we appreciate that it's literally thousands of pounds of plastic and steel traveling at rates to create enough kinetic energy to turn you into soup. Distracted driving causes thousands of accidents every year and the solution is simple: quit purposefully distracting yourself while driving. Quit making the conscious decision to not fully pay attention while operating a speeding ball of death.

That time I was instructing a class about HIV/AIDS and a guy chimed in with, "Yeah, that's why I don't brush my teeth before giving oral sex; the bristles from the tooth brush can cut small holes in your mouth and create a chance for the disease to be transferred." I seriously didn't know what to say except, "Oooo....kay..." and just moved on with the lecture.

Or that time I was instructing a class around Halloween, and one of the TA's came in dressed as a clown, and we found out who has an extreme clown phobia. (to be fair, this was around the time when killer clowns somehow made a comeback and started terrorizing certain areas). I'm not sure we did too many clown costumes after that year.

Or the time I had a student fall asleep during a demonstration (we usually demoed out the new modality on the first day of each class to give the students a preview of what they'd be learning) which isn't all that terrible, but he wouldn't admit to being asleep and then doubled down on preferring to watch with his eyes closed. Now, if you fall asleep during a demo, I get it. The music's relaxing, its dark, you're watching the equivalent of a slow, rhythmic dance and you're in a comfortable position—I get it (we got our fair share of snoring in mediation classes too). When this happens, I would just politely ask them to wake up and stand if they need to. But I wasn't prepared for the argument of, "I prefer to watch with my eyes closed." I also wasn't prepared for him to get hostile either. Luckily, he eventually stormed out of the classroom. *Snowflake millennials!!*

Or how 'bout that student that failed out of the entire massage program (that's a bill of about $13,000) because she didn't want to attempt the CPR hands-on final. To be clear, she didn't want to get on the ground to perform basic CPR on a mannequin with proper sanitation equipment present, so she chose to fail out of the ENTIRE program. She looked me right in the eyes and said, "I'd just let them die anyways."

Now, as a bystander, yeah, you don't have to get into anyone's business if you don't want to. It's sad, but even getting involved with the best of intentions may get you in trouble. Sure, there's good Samaritan laws, but it seems like more and more good people that stop to help are getting themselves into less than

134

preferable situations (recently had a German friend inform me that he was told when he was getting his driver's license, to drive to the next gas station and phone for help if he saw someone in need. Let the authorities handle it to ensure your safety. Unfortunately, pirates, scammers, and overall wackjobs are still a thing in the 21st century.). So, you have that choice as a bystander. But as a massage therapist in the middle of a session, no, the client is our responsibility. You don't have a choice but to get involved. You can't just be like, "Uhhh…Imma go on break." The client on the table is our sole responsibility. The chances of something happening are so slim, but if something did happen in a session, I wouldn't want the girl who's cool with me dying to be working on me.

When we were clearing out our office and switching over to a strictly mobile service, we had a yard sale. Our location was a bit odd, you could only park in the designated parking areas or your car could easily get stuck. So, we had this army vet pull up in a truck, and I politely asked him to park in the appropriate parking area. He starts going off about how I'm an idiot for not letting him park in the spot that says no parking. So, I shrug my shoulders and send him on through. Like, 30 seconds later he's cursing and shouting up a storm because he's stuck. Everyone's staring and I can't stop laughing. He eventually was able to back out of the rut but then still refused to pull into the parking area to turn around or park. He just reversed his way out of site, like that meant he won or something?

I once worked for a spa and some guy called in asking if the girls could line up for him so he could pick. Don't be trash. Don't be like this guy.

———————

Student once asked me if it hurt more to be kicked in the balls or the vagina (this is in adult education, mind you). Believe it or not, I have never been kicked in my vagina. For, I do not have a vagina.

But from the looks of it, most everything hurts more for a woman, just generally speaking. Except for Peggy Hill from the show 'King of the Hill', she can get kicked in the vagina all day and not even feel it. *"That's my purse! I don't know you!"*

———————

The time the assistant manager at a spa I worked at tried to get me to admit I smoked marijuana by telling me all the times he smoked it and what he liked to do while high. I didn't smoke the stuff (my entire life people have thought I've smoked pot, even when I was kid. I remember being ten and being yelled at by an adult because I "looked high". It stems from me having giant, circus like eyes and having been made fun of for it. I would always squint to hide my melon sized eyeballs. Seriously, I have goofy anime eyes. Jacob Holly who did the cover for the book did a fantastic job at making me look relatively normal.) and didn't say anything to even acknowledge his presence, but I did tell our boss about the conversation and how unprofessional it was.

BTW, just to help frame the story here a little better. The assistant manager was the kind of guy who you could say his name out loud and someone would answer back, "now you be careful 'round him." Yeah, he also had a list of people he wanted to fire, he just left it out for people to see.

———————

Also had another assistant manager at a chiropractic clinic that, no joke, read text messages from her alcoholic husband apologizing for being an alcoholic. I wish him the best of luck and hope he gets help, of course, but sitting through that was the absolute most awkward thing I've ever had to sit through. I would rather tell the class two truths and a lie every day for the rest of my life then sit through another second of that. And I mean, it's not like the whole clinic was eavesdropping, intruding on her privacy; she started off our team meeting with this—no one asked. No one also said anything over the few minutes it took her to read all these aloud. And we all just kind of moved on afterwards like that was a total normal thing to do. That day still perplexes me.

———————

Serious note for a sec. I once worked with a recovering alcoholic. We didn't always get along, but I always did, and still do, root for her. Originally this part of the book was going to be about all the freak outs she had but I rather say if you're struggling with something and need a friend—look me up, I'm here for you.

Okay, back to less serious notes.

———————

Fun fact about me, I'm actually one of the few men with a maiden name. (Name that movie!)

———————

Once worked with a guy who had been a massage therapist for 13 years and couldn't set up a massage table. Imagine being in a field for over a decade and not knowing how to do something that you learn your first week. How the hell do you survive? That's like being a pilot for 13 years and not knowing how to take off, it's a crucial part to the practice.

For those of you wondering what he did versus proper technique:

> What he did (what you don't do): You do not unfold your table on its side then fling it into the air and whip down onto all fours. This was actually his reasoning for not doing mobile massage, "it's too hard on the table."

> Proper technique (what you should do): You should unfold your table on its side, then find one of two the legs touching the floor. Place your foot at the bottom of one of those legs and just lean back slightly. The leg will catch into the floor and the table will just tilt until it's on all fours. Easy, peasy, lemon squeezy.

———————

Was supervising student massage therapists at an expo and this lady started yelling at me because the school I worked for wouldn't hire her as an instructor because she didn't have any massage experience. She had a master's degree in teaching, but no massage experience, and this was my fault. Somehow. I've never felt more like a child in my whole life. I just sat there and took it like it was actually my fault that she couldn't get hired for a job that required experience in its respective field. Just nuts man. *ThIs GeNeRaTiOn WaNtS eVeRyThInG hAnDeD tO tHeM. DeR dE dEr.De DeR.*

———————

I worked with a gal whose house burned down. I always tried to make sure she had the same room at work for some sense of regularity. We hired a new guy that took her room his first day and no joke, I almost had to fight him to get him move one room over. He was upset because he had to move a lotion bottle and some business cards.

This same guy threw our entire team under the bus one day, or at least he tried—my wife stood up while he was talking and shouted his name followed by a thunderous, "NO!" That's all she said, and that boy tucked tail and changed his whole story. I re-fell in love with her that day.

If you want to be a massage therapist, you can do it. I bet, nay guarantee, you even have the potential to be better than me. I've worked with members of the UFC, NFL, MLB and US Special Forces and I know for a fact that you can make me look like a tinker toy.

You work a lot with your hands in this field, obviously. I never knew my birth mother growing up but approaching my 30th trip around the sun—I met her. For the first time, I met my mom. One of the first things she said to me was, "Good God son, how do you do massage with such little hands?" I had gone over in my head for decades about what I would say to her if I ever met her, but I hadn't planned on that. No Disney movie prepared me for this.

I look like the freakin' guy from those Burger King commercials, *"They're not that tiny." "THEY ARE THAT TINY."*

So yes, if I don't just survive, but thrive in a field that requires a professional look and awesome hand strength with my freakishly small hands and giant, anime like eyeballs then you'll do just fine…oh, might I also mention that there's joints in my thumbs that never fully developed either. They're there, they just have about a third of the range of motion that normal thumbs should have (and again, about half the size). For example, I'm sure you can take the tip of your thumb and touch the base of your pinky—not me. I can struggle and get close, but just can't. So, trust me, if my girlish, feeble, hands can manage, then I know yours can.

Also, my head is just big. Most hat companies don't even make sizes for my gargantuan head. So, just imagine when I got my first pair of glasses, that poor optometrist was like, *"What in the hell are you?!"*

If I can do it, you can do it.

(fun fact about me, I once took first in two categories and second in three categories during a world's martial arts tournament. As you can see above, I'm working with a Frankenstein body here, so, if I can do it, you can do it. Believe me, you got this.)

———————

When I worked at the school, at one point there was a transition in education managers. A colleague of mine was unanimously voted to **not** be the next manager. Every day he came in and basically told us he would either quit or fire us. Not the most convincing case I've heard for a promotion, but Goddamn did I appreciate his effort...I—I think.

———————

I was once invited to an energy share by a chiropractor. At this energy share, we would all work on each other with our different disciplines and introduce new people to our techniques and the world of energetic healing. Regardless if you believed in the stuff or not, it was a free class with the intent of just spreading good and no one ever left angry. For some, it was the exact spark of hope that they needed. But, before we got started, we all went around the room and introduced ourselves and the modality we'd be sharing. Everyone in the room (there was about 15 of us) except for me and the chiropractor holding the event were students of this one woman who practiced reiki. I practice chi gong (qigong, chikung). I don't know what her problem was, but she tried to put me down several times about my practice. Most energy modalities are under the umbrella of chi gong (chi = energy, gong = work, it literally means energy work), so it really made no difference to me. Call it what you want. After a few of these attempts though, the chiropractor holding the event interrupted her and said, "last year I went to the birthplace of reiki—Japan. It was there I spoke with the Grandmaster and asked him of the difference between chi gong and reiki. He laughed and said, 'reiki is chi gong repackaged for American tourists.'" Then the chiropractor, the students, and I had a good laugh. The reiki master did not.

Of course, this story isn't meant to bash reiki masters or their discipline, but this lady was the type of person to take advantage of people and their wallets. When you see dollar signs when helping someone, you've already doomed your practice.

––––––––––––

Why were students always stopping me and asking me superficial (near dumb) questions when I was on a mad dash to the restroom? Did they somehow take pleasure in watching my pee-pee-dance?

––––––––––––

Had an instructor in school tell us not to give our very best massage because we could fix the issue and not see repeat clients. DO NOT do this if you're an aspiring massage therapist. First off, I don't even know how one would gauge this. And Secondly, anything lower than you best work is garbage and won't incite repeat clients anyways.

––––––––––––

If you were injured/sick and were unable to let a student practice on you, then you would be asked to sign out of class. The massage school had some odd standards (more on that in a second), if you were unable to do the work, they made you leave only to make up your attendance in a class you didn't need (e.g. injury massage class to an acupressure class. Don't ask me why they thought this policy would work, but in the end, I guess it didn't). With all this in mind, I had a student present with a hernia (tear in the abdominal wall, allowing insides to protrude out) and we were doing DEEP abdominal work that day. There was no way this person was getting on the table. I asked her to sign out and she responded with, "but you let me stay last time and I had a hernia then." Before I got caught up in this back n' forth nonsense, I walked her to the director and explained the situation. To my surprise I had to apologize to her to keep my job. Although I was acting within proper protocol, I was still in the wrong. She felt it was a "power trip" and felt like I was being prejudice—so I was forced to apologize, and she got to sit in class with a smug grin.

Now, to be clear here, I think she should've been able to sit in class with an injury to begin with. Didn't bother me one bit if a student was taking notes on bodywork and still actively learning, in fact, I pushed for it during staff meetings. But again, what's with the double standard? Why does she get to have her way while so many other students got stiffed?

Not to mention, this also made it much harder for all the other instructors to have consistency in their classrooms. You let one student get away with it because she threw a fit, then anyone who throws a fit can get away with it. Not just that, but if it's that policy, then it can be any policy. But upper management cared far more about their numbers (students enrolled and the money they bring with them) v. their policies. Which leads me to my next point...

I was an instructor at the massage school, I was asked to be 'a body on the table'. This normally meant that the person working on you was a taking a retest for a hands-on final and/or could potentially harm someone with their questionable technique. They normally tested on other students, but with ample risk present you'd turn to a staff member to be tested on. As I was on the table, none of the trigger point techniques felt right and I would've definitely failed him, but I wasn't testing him. It was the day of his (potential) graduation and the instructor administering the testing didn't want him to fail the program being so close to the finish line (you only got so many retakes before they dropped you altogether). So, she passed him and said, "just make sure you don't work trigger points on anyone." That's like asking a chef to not use a knife— trigger point is a massage therapist's bread and butter. Without that you might as well not even get started.

The same student called the instructor about a year later because he was going into a massage interview and needed to know how to do massage. He was totally unprepared and that was on her. There are no shortcuts in life, just short expectations.

By the way, this wasn't the only time I saw something like this happen.

I used to TA for that same lady (from the story above) before I became an instructor. As I was walking into my first class to teach (literally my first class as an instructor), she pulls me aside and tells me how much the national director thinks I should be fired and I'm an embarrassment to the school and this n' that— I had demoed some techniques earlier that day that apparently weren't up to their standards. I'm already nervous walking into my first class, then she lays this on me.

(The reality of the situation was the corporate team was pretty useless and ruffled feathers as part of the act. They'd show up to your campus and play 'big brother is watching you' to scare your team into doing their jobs better. Rarely, did they ever offer advice and of that advice, it was rarely useful. I remember one of the corporate team members tried recording a draping video so the chain of schools could have a reference—it was literally the worst draping I'd ever seen and I taught the newbies how to drape. There was another corporate member who asked us why we thought we had poor attendance. Many students mentioned to us they were having transportation issues. He then suggested we had attendance issues not because students had issues finding rides to class, but rather because we believed students didn't have proper transportation. Let that sink in, he told us people weren't showing up because we didn't think they had cars when they actually didn't have cars. But if we just thought them to be liars, it made it so. I love the mental gymnastics of corporate shills.)

I knew she must've felt so good about it too, because later after the class the education manager came up to me and told me that that instructor should've never said anything to me, it wasn't her job and I'm doing fine. Which told me the instructor sought the approval of the education manager by bragging to her after the beratement. Wish I could've been there when that grin was wiped off her face.

———————

Or how 'bout that time I was having heart problems (nothing serious), so I went to hospital and was instructed to take time off of work. I managed to get one day and even then, someone who I covered for when they were on maternity leave had the gull to guilt trip me about covering for me while I was out for a day. I think women should get ample maternity leave, but it's always been odd to me that you can cover for someone for months at a time and they come back like you still owe them something.

When you enroll in massage school, time is taken to teach you basic anatomical terms such as "superior v. inferior" means "up v. down", "lateral v. medial" means "sides v. middle", "anterior v. posterior" means "front v. back"; foundational information. It comes in handy later when you're learning more in-depth anatomical concepts. With that in mind, I once had a student who was fresh out of the army special forces tell me that when he was in the field reporting an injury, they had a system of labeling only for one side of the body and assuming it was the other side if unlabeled. Example: If the injury was located on the hand, and it was labeled 'posterior hand', the medic would check the **back** of the hand. But if it was just labeled as 'hand', then the medic would check the front of the hand, assuming it wasn't the back—even without the word 'anterior' present.

When I responded to his comment, little did I know he was trying to set up the argument of *everyone in the class should only learn posterior and not anterior because that's how they spoke in the army during a fire fight*. Like, not even learn it at all, just stick to one side of the body and anything you don't know, just assume it's the opposite direction. And it's not like this was a quick back n' forth of, "Hey, here's a dumb idea." Then, "We're not doing that. That's dumb. Moving on." I seriously had to stop the entire class for about 10 minutes and explain to this guy, multiple times, that's not how it works. No one is paying $13,000 to learn half the material because you were in the army.

Then to make matters worse, someone else in the class chimed in. Started going off about how I'm not getting the first guy and then proceeded to repeat everything he said, with a crescendoing voice. Then started ranting about how you can't just live with one kidney. Most people can, but there was no convincing her of that—and I didn't even know how we got there.

This soon turned into a Colosseum style gladiator fight. Picture this, I'm at the front of the class and literally the two people directly in front of me are causing all this chaos, with 40+ people surrounding us. The two of them screaming all while sporting a devilish, unwavering stare—that physical therapist type of stare (if you didn't get that then read the chapter "LMT's V. DPT's: Why Are They Such Dicks to Us?"). Spoiler alert, they didn't win that argument and soon dropped from the program after that.

Or how 'bout that time I got a full body cramp on the way to work, then missed a week. I don't take Day/Nyquil because of this incident. Originally, I had just missed work for a day because of the flu. Waking up the next day I still didn't feel very well but wasn't given permission to miss another shift (my benevolent overloads were not pleased). So, I loaded up on medication and made my way to work. On the way, I felt my fingers start to tingle along with my lips. Then it made its way up from my fingers and down from my lips towards my chest. Just as I pulled into the parking lot, the tingles turned to sharp stabbing pains as my body contracted and contorted. My vision blurred and my breathing became restricted. I fell out of my truck onto the hot pavement—Phoenix pavement in the summer. The burning sensation was enough motivation to get up off the ground, though. I fumbled my way into the office where my wife was at; I hated letting her see me like that. Even with doctors on staff, there wasn't much to do but wait it out. It took a few hours before the pain left and I could fully move again. Then I slept for about 15 hours a day for the next week. Like I said, I don't take Day/Nyquil anyone.

I also don't get sick as much now that I don't work in a clinic. Even being in peoples' home with sick kids, I don't get sick as often. Keep your hands away from your face and keep your mind away from negative workspaces, it'll do wonders for your health.

―――――――

Used to work with a guy that would take his hour lunch, then come back with a lunch and sit there for another hour on the clock and eat—freakin' legend, man. Freakin' legend.

―――――――

Worked with a lady that would leave her radio on when she left for the day, so when she came in late the next morning, people would assume she had been there, but they just couldn't find her. She could normally just slip in the back or act like she had been doing some marketing out on the town if someone did see her come in. *Is it possible to learn this power?* (name that movie!)

―――――――

Once I finished the first program of massage training, I had the option to continue my education with an advanced program that would be held at a different campus. There was already this odd feud between the two campuses (yeah, even in massage somehow—who wudda thunk?), so it didn't help that I immediately got off on the wrong foot with one of the instructors there. I found his classes boring and unproductive and I expressed that thought thoroughly. He took offense to my opinions of him (which again, to clarify, were not positive. I would've disapproved of me too) and stopped talking to me. Like, would refuse to even acknowledge my presence. I could literally keep pace beside him trying to grab his attention and he would just keep walking. It was like out of a movie. Regardless, he had to acknowledge me at the graduation ceremony for being one of two students to nab a 4.0 in the program. *Ha!*

―――――――

I was on a radio show with 2 million people listening and I thought it went well. It was a simple interview about bodywork and my career, only about 10 minutes or so. As we got off the air, I asked the DJ how I did. He responded with, "Well, you didn't stutter. So, there's that. We'll send you a copy of the show and if you're brave enough, you can listen to it." Then he hung up. They never sent it. My ego ruptured like a pinata.

So, when you do chair massage at an event, typically you don't use lotion and you just use a lot of non-gliding techniques for the session instead. I was at an event with a guy who didn't wash his hands when massaging with lotion—hand sanitizer normally suffices at an event, but it is essential to wash your hands with soap and water after a lotion application. But he just kept compacting lotion on top of lotion from person to person until there was this layer of dead skin he had accumulated from the crowd, caked across his hands. *Gaaah...* the worst part was he then had the audacity to tell me he was going to steal all my clients. *HA! Coming from the guy who doesn't even wash his hands. HA!*

We once made the mistake of advertising in a certain Facebook group that we do free chair massage at events. Dozens upon dozens of requests came flooding in inquiring about our free massage chair after that. Notice the slight but crucial difference between the two. Free chair massage v. free massage chair—we were not giving away any massage chairs, but yet somehow, we chummed the waters and attracted the attention of...well...*them. They who do not read, but still comment.*

We once had a student call the massage board and they apparently were told that they didn't have to complete any clinical intern hours to get licensed. For you see, after so many weeks of training, you start a clinical internship at the school on the weekends. This part in the process is vital and was taken very seriously. Missing even one day would result in a failure of the entire program. But it does take a toll being at an intern level. Not making money and working is not a position some people can manage well. So, I don't blame her for trying to get out of it, but sadly, it was concluded with her demise. Even after the school confirmed with her that she needed so many hours in her internship to graduate, she called their bluff and was dropped from the program like a sack of potatoes.

———————

After I successfully finished teaching my first big course (it was a foundational course), one of my fellow instructors came up to me and mentioned that the rest of team was sure I was going to fail but to their surprise I did great instead. *Thanks, I-I guess…?* But it begs the question: if you were so certain I was going to fail, then why didn't you or anyone else on the team make any effort to help? For the same reason that the head of student services never completely taught her two assistants how to fully do their or her job—Ding! Ding! Ding! Ding! Ding! Job security, baby. The worse I do, the better they look and the harder their job looks. Which in turn, makes the school that much more dependent on them. If in the event cuts do need to be made, they'll cut those who know less and have proven a faultier track record. Basically, the students who pay thousands of dollars to be in the classroom were nothing more than pawns in a giant pissing contest (I rather prefer the term 'peeing races' by the way. Name that reference!).

———————

We used to hand out an assignment the first week of massage school that would ask about hypothetical situations and how you would react to them (e.g., how would you respond if a client wanted to date you or how would you respond if a client became aggressive) and then later we would go over these scenarios and what you should've done. This one student had an issue with the assignment. She was one of those baby boomers that would constantly talk trash about how lazy young people are then throw a fit anytime she was asked to do anything at all—she actually said to me once that she'd "forgotten more stuff than I'll ever learn".

When the assignment was due, she brought me her 'finished ' product and told me that she purposefully answered some of the questions incorrectly because, "if I was going to waste her time then she was going to waste mine" and if I didn't catch ALL of her mistakes then she was going to complain to the director of the school. Yeah, she was an absolute treat to have around.

So, I graded her paper like any other and gave her a crap score for all her wrong answers. How's the old expression go? Play stupid games, win stupid prizes.

I still wonder what her whole thought process was and if she was really proud of that plan. Like, she probably stayed up all night thinking about that one. I'm just not impressed anymore by the purposefully stupid.

Long live the troll, though, I guess.

––––––––––––

When I graduated from massage school, I was employed at a grocery store. I managed the frozen food department and would commonly help out in other departments. On one of my last days being employed there, I helped in the liquor department. The boxes they ship alcohol in are thicker than other boxes used throughout the store. Between that and not paying attention, I stacked the box ready to cut it's top off, and when I did the box cutter skipped out of its groove and continued the slice WHILE IN MY FREAKING THUMB. I cut myself from the base to the tip of my thumb—I thought my massage career was done before it started. Luckily, I'm just as tough as I am ugly, so I powered through. You can hardly see the scar now.

When I first entered my instructing position at the massage school, I was informed to not release any of my personal contact information to the students. Instead, I would have an office line I would give out. Overzealous in my youth, it didn't make sense to me and I didn't care to listen. I was rarely around my office phone and wanted students to be able to reach me—so I gave out my personal cell and email. Seemed harmless enough and my intent was good, but after some time I realized that was a grave mistake.

Humble brag time. Unfortunately, this happened to me more than once; a student becoming infatuated with me and begins stalking me. Notable moments include:

Another student pulling me aside to tell me that her friend has loads of pictures of me of her phone—pictures I didn't know she took. Some even from that day.

A student started popping up at places I'd be planning to go. Basically, anywhere I had posted about on social media. (#creepy).

Another student that I had an argument with during school, has made multiple attempts to harass me post-graduation. Even made up this whole story about how I tried sabotaging his career by influencing the massage board to delay or revoke his license. It's like having an evil villain just drop into your life for no good reason. Odd thing is—he's even applied for a job. (I'm not going to lie, my first reaction was to hire him and send him to empty lots across town until he quit, but that's just not my style.)

The school's education manager and director pulled me aside once to ask my side of the story and then to skip town for the weekend. Apparently, a student came to them confessing her undying, immortal love for me. Which lead them to questioning me about my involvement with her, I had no idea what was happening. They ended the line of questioning by reassuring me I did nothing wrong, then told me to go somewhere for weekend and not tell anyone where I was going (seriously, like in the movies). "*You like camping, right? Why don't you take a nice trip this weekend? In fact, go ahead and leave now. Take the rest of the day off.*" My theory is during her confession of undying love, she also mentioned a few threats to my safety as well.

What can I say? I'm just all that and a bag of potato chips.

———————

Someone once called me the "Bob Ross of massage" because of how I taught. One of the biggest compliments I think I'll ever receive. The only other compliment I've heard that even comes to that is "As sure as the sun will rise, Raf will rise for work." Like, daaaaamn, makin' a brown man blush over here.

———————

When I was in massage school, we had a toy drive for the children's hospital. It was being presented by the education manager. One of my classmates raised his hand and asked, "Should we not buy the game 'Operation' then?" and she replied with a straight face, "Wow. You have a dark sense of humor. No, you should not buy the game 'Operation' for the kids at the children's hospital."

———————

When I was in massage school, a classmate of mine had a really hard time. She was a single mother just trying to make a good life for her and her kids. Then one day, someone steals her car and crashes it, destroying it and everything inside—including her massage manuals and table. Basically, that person squashed any chance of success for her in the program. If you can't study and practice, then you won't make it. She couldn't afford a new set of books and a table, let alone another car; she was going to have to drop from the program and abandon a wonderful opportunity. I wasn't cool with that. I hate seeing someone trying to do good get beat down. It makes me uncomfortable. So, I got a group of classmates together and we reached out for donations, I told them I'd cover whatever the difference was for the books and table and I'd give her a ride to and from school from then on out. It was a success; we covered the cost for over $500 in material. We got her used manuals, a used table, and she wouldn't have to pay any gas money to get to and from school. It wasn't perfect but at least she had a fighting chance now.

We graduated from that program and even went on to an advanced massage program together. Same thing there; picked her up (and even another gal) every day to get her to class and didn't charge her for gas. I was just happy to see someone trying to make a better life for themselves and their family. It's refreshing to see that dreams do come true. After we graduated that program, there was no more training to be had, and it was time to go our separate ways and enter the real world. That's—that's when she told me the truth.

No one stole her car, but someone did crash it. She was drunk behind the wheel and rammed her vehicle into one of those concrete poles that are there to stop morons just like her from crashing into a building or a lake. She fled the scene with help from another classmate. Picked her up and dropped her off at home. Together, they fabricated the story and took advantage of an entire class for over a year. I still remember that grin on her face when she told me the police questioned her later that night and she was still drunk but held it together enough to convince them that she didn't know her vehicle was gone.

Its moments like that that really make you think. For a while after, I had the words of Walter Kovac (aka Rorschach) stuck in my head, "The accumulated filth…will foam up around their waists and all the…politicians will look up and shout 'Save us!' And I'll whisper 'No'." (Watchmen, 1986)

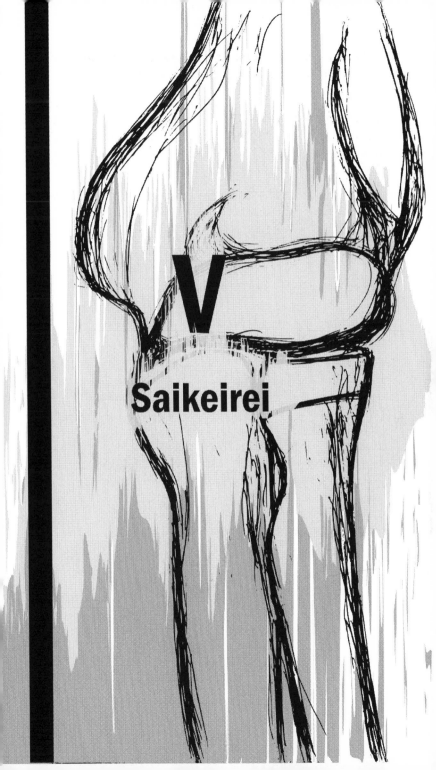

V
Saikeirei

Most Sincerely, Thank You

You made it! You read the whole thing! Iron has met velvet, student has become sensei, the immovable has been moved, the unstoppable stopped, and the titan has been fed and conquered. Now, **I bow to you**. Most sincerely, thank you for taking the time to read my book (or at least for playing into your curiosity when you noticed that PART V was redacted from the table and contents and skipping your way here). A million thank you's to you, my wonderful reader, and may just as much good fortune come your way. I am humbled to have had you as an audience and I hope you enjoyed the read. It is an honor to be of service to you. Thank you, thank you for your time. Most gratitude for your energy. And I am grateful for you listening to my five crying tigers.

But if it's not too forward of me, I'd like to also offer a piece of advice along with my appreciation: **live your life.** Like really live it. Do those things that you keep talking about. Do those things that spark happiness deep within you but are then vanquished by '*rational*' thought. Even if it's just hanging out playing videos from when you were a kid; do it. Take one step towards your goal and don't waste another second. You don't have to live an exciting life to live a happy one, but you still have to live it. I'd rather be the man that tried and failed, then the man that never tried at all. I love you. You got this. Don't let the graveyard be the resting place of your ideas and ventures, for you must always remember that all this will end someday. And it can end…

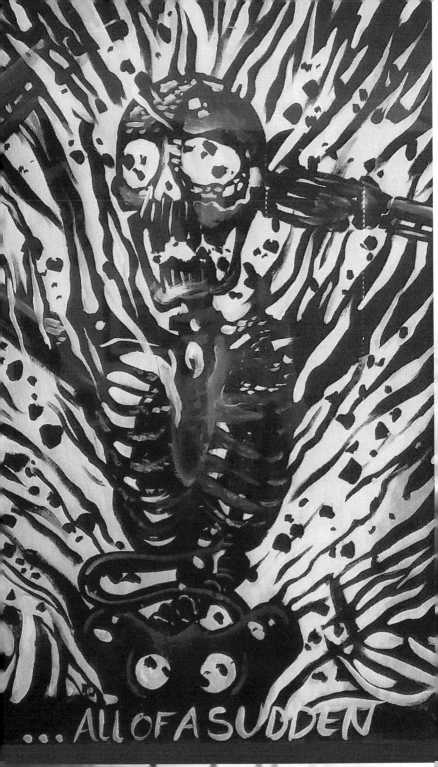

*(A little background on the painting: I came across Denise and her work when I was on tour with a rock band through California. We stopped at a tattoo shop where they were having an art contest. The theme of the contest revolved around how the world would end. This was the only one of its kind. All the other depicted asteroids, or a virus, or nuclear warfare, or Cthulhu, but this was the only piece of work that gave no explanation— just that it would happen and without notice. Spontaneous combustion with no rhyme or reason. It was the first time a painting caused me to have an emotional reaction. It moved me and still moves me. An awesome reminder to not waste your time here. Thank you, **Denise T. Pinto**, for your work and awesome talent.)*

Oh yeah, and one more thing…always, always remember, to be safe and stay safe, be awesome and stay awesome. Have a beautiful day everyone. Much love.

The Official Five Crying Tigers Spit, Chat, Jive and Jabber

By Declan "Haze Thy Puppetmaster" Cooney

Who is this mystery? This mist, I see
Gifted misery, you can check the history
Let me clear the air, be fair and square
Aware that we're fragile, handle with care
These lives we touch, and the pressure placed
There's a time for haste, and no time to waste
Impressive is the desire of the youth to mend
From fricative beginnings, to their fear of the end
Some resist the current created by schools
Of fishes with wishes of riches and jewels
Hands, indicative of tools
Shams, implicative fools
And fluid the rules, in ruinous coups
As we rue insidious mistakes that we choose
But students imbue new air to the flame
Realized anew, perspectives exchanged
Me, defective and maimed
He, respectful and sane
How does one regenerate passion and grace?
After falling from positive action and faith?
Enjoying reciprocation, our own elixirs we chug
It is the least we can do, giving Atlas a shrug
The power of touch has the power to heal
Different hands for different needs, depending on pain that we feel

If I had ultimate power, would I corrupt it
Be decisive in my healing, yet divisive enough that

Money would make a difference in who saw my light
Judge not lest ye be judged, unless the profit is right
Worldly problems sink into the facets of life
Fear-mongering, racism, and sexism alike
Some places tradition has been sequestered and muted
Other places it's losers whose campaigns' are rebooted
There are grains of truth in all things refuted
So please understand that this industry is diluted
With sexual preference, and bias toward race
Corporate boots on small businesses faces
It is up to us to erase this baseless way of innateness
Clear the slate, for those making their way from the shade
This is not just a song, it is a plea for alliances
Apply your mind and might and fight for righteousness
Follow the light, find yourself aligned with this
Pine for this, a time when minds will shift
This guy is a gift, his shine is so slick
Take a page from his book, and evade the tricks
Engage with your kids, and sustain the love that pervades
In this business we aid those weary from time as they fade
Despite relaxation and range restoration
Compassionate engagement offers a range of creation
It brings us together from all parts of the globe
Allowing peaceful surrender, prone and disrobed
Ambassadors of Altruism, Touch, and Trust
Outnumber the imposters who are publicly trussed
As a public we must protect our healers and weak
From the ever vile ones, it is oppression they seek
Licensed and trained, we honor your worth
Higher standards are sought by the people of Earth

Credits

1. 'Vertebrae' by Raf and Linda King. Inspired by the photo 'Brown Bone' by Meta Zahren.
2. 'Brain' by Raf and Linda King. Inspired by the photo "Brown Brain" by Robina Weermeijer.
3. 'Heart' by Raf and Linda King. Inspired by the photo "Orange Heart Décor" by Robina Weermeijer.
4. 'Ribcage' by Raf and Linda King. Inspired by the photo "Animal Bone Photography" by Meta Zahren('Joint' by Raf and Linda King.
5. 'Joint' by Raf and Linda King.
6. 'All of a Sudden' by Denise T. Pinto.
7. 'The Official Five Crying Tigers Spit, Chat, Jive and Jabber' by Declan "Haze Thy Puppetmaster" Cooney.

Made in the USA
Columbia, SC
23 December 2019